BERLIN
Like a Local

DK EYEWITNESS

BERLIN
Like a Local

BY THE PEOPLE WHO CALL IT HOME

Contents

EAT

DRINK

SHOP

ARTS & CULTURE

meet the locals

MARLEN JACOBSHAGEN

Having worked on several city guides, German content creator Marlen knows Berlin like the back of her hand. Work aside, she loves cycling around on her creaky bike in search of new vegan foods to try. Though Marlen misses her coastal hometown Lübeck at times, a cold beer by the lake is a quick remedy.

ALEXANDER RENNIE

South London-born Alex made the switch to Berlin in 2014 to study, and has stayed firmly put since. When not juggling his passion for writing with a career in content marketing, Alex is digging crates at second-hand record shops, getting lost in Berlin's glorious nature or throwing the odd shape on one of its dusty dance floors.

BARBARA WOOLSEY

Born in Canada, Barbara's called Berlin home for nearly a decade now and couldn't imagine living elsewhere. Between working as a journalist and completing her Masters, she's dancing at open-airs, shopping at markets and hunting for her next favourite craft beer.

Berlin

WELCOME TO THE CITY

People flock to Berlin to live true to themselves. This is a place where starry-eyed artists get inspired in graffitied alleys, LGBTQ+ folks cuddle their partners in public and immigrants find refuge in the city's unadulterated freedom. Born Berliners are a rare breed; rather, Berlin is a patchwork of nonconformists and hedonists from far and wide. And despite their (many) differences, they're bound by tolerance and solidarity. Gentrifying forces may brew but Berliners fiercely defend their lifestyle and one another, whether scaring off Google from opening a campus or rallying for renters' rights.

This is a city of survivors, after all. A difficult past is a canvas for today's shabby chic aesthetic – the Berlin Wall is constantly reinvented with new art, bomb shelters become decadent clubs and disused industrial estates turn into lush parks. Creativity is the backbone of this ever-changing city. Your favourite

mural, underground party or apartment contract may disappear in a second, but Berliners roll with the punches. They know that every change brings something new to discover, whether it's a hidden pop-up restaurant or a boundary-pushing bookstore.

In a city that's always redefining itself, getting to know all of its facets isn't easy. That's where this book comes in. We know how Berliners spend their time, from shedding their inhibitions (and wardrobe) at sex-positive nights to getting their fix of the ultimate döner kebab. Of course, these pages can never capture such a diverse, spontaneity-driven city entirely. Instead, this book celebrates snapshots of local life and inspires you to choose your own adventure.

Whether you're a seasoned Berliner sussing out the city's secrets or seeking to strike beyond the iconic sights, this book will help you embrace the weird and wonderful energy at Berlin's heart.

Liked by the locals

"In Berlin, anything goes as long as you respect others. That unbridled freedom makes it a haven for self-expression and nonconformity – beloved by creative types, queer folks and free spirits from all backgrounds and stripes."

BARBARA WOOLSEY, TRAVEL WRITER

Something is always afoot in this vibrant city. Think alfresco parties in the summer, spa soaks in the autumn and festive markets in the winter.

Berlin
THROUGH THE YEAR

SPRING

MARKETS GALORE
Marking the transition from winter to spring is the return of the city's beloved markets. Peddlers set up their stalls with vintage treasures and tasty treats, perfect for a day's mooch.

THE GREAT OUTDOORS
Surviving the brittle winter makes spring that much sweeter. Joggers return to the streets, cyclists hit the roads en masse and Sunday *Spaziergänge* (strolls) become much more appealing.

BEER GARDENING
The moment Berliners have been waiting for since late September finally arrives: the reopening of beer gardens.

Across the city, young and old gather on benches, toasting to longer evenings with frothy beers.

SUMMER

LAKE LIVING
You're not a proper Berliner until you've spent summer weekends cooling off at a glacial lake. Friends rent motorized rafts to party on the water, swimmers embrace nature and sunbathers bare all in the spirit of FKK (free body culture).

PARTY WITH PRIDE
Out-and-proud Berliners and their allies fly rainbow flags at celebrations throughout summer. June sees the streets around Nollendorfplatz come alive with the Lesbian and Gay City

Festival and July draws crowds who dance all the way to Brandenburger Tor for the Christopher Street Day parade.

ALFRESCO ANTICS
Retreating indoors in the summer is practically unheard of. Days are spent tending to BBQs and drinking *Späti*-bought beers in parks before heading to an open-air club to dance.

OUTDOOR CINEMAS
Freiluftkinos (open-air cinemas) pop up in parks and old courtyards as soon as balmy nights hit. Enjoying a classic under the stars is a joyous pastime.

AUTUMN

CULTURAL TOURS
Faced with cooler weather and fading summer memories, locals keep their spirits high with a new cultural season. Performing arts programmes get underway with gusto, and museums provide perfect rainy day shelter.

LEAFY WALKS
Come autumn, weekends at the lakes are swapped for long walks. Tiergarten *(p170)* is a favourite spot to soak up the season's fiery auburn hues, while Grunewald *(p188)* is ideal for a day of lush forest walks.

PAMPER TIME
Spa culture starts to heat up in winter, with Berliners looking to stave off the grey days and vitamin D deficit.

WINTER

RAVE CAVES
Berlin's dark winters are a drag, so locals retreat into the city's world-class (albeit just as dark) clubs to escape. With parties lasting all weekend, it's easy to forget about the elements outside.

CHRISTMAS MARKETS
Berliners never tire of December's famed *Weihnachtsmärkte* – and why would they, with *Glühwein* (mulled wine), handmade gifts and festive cheer?

FESTIVAL FUN
A packed, creative events calendar kicks off the new year in style. Fashion Week in January tempts the renewal of wardrobes, while Berlinale in February offers inspiration (and an excuse to cosy up and watch a film or five).

There's an art to being a Berliner, from the dos and don'ts in the club queue to negotiating the city's vast streets. Here's a breakdown of all you need to know.

Berlin
KNOW-HOW

For a directory of health and safety resources, safe spaces and accessibility information, turn to page 190. For everything else, read on.

EAT
Eating on the hoof is standard in Berlin, and much-loved *Imbisse* (snack kiosks) are visited before, during and after work. That's not to say sit-down affairs are overlooked. Leisurely brunches are a weekend fixture, and spots start filling up from around 11am. Locals love to eat dinner out, too, so much so that booking ahead is a must, especially when it comes to uber-trendy joints (of which there are many).

DRINK
If anything fuels creative sessions, it's coffee; the third-wave revolution is big business here, and so is enjoying a brew in a cool café. As for alcohol, the scene is a mix of upmarket joints and cheap dives. Most places only close when the crowds thin out, so drinking happens at a slower pace – it's rare to see anyone really drunk.

Public drinking is also legal, and buying beers from a *Späti* (convenience store) to drink in a park is a pastime.

SHOP
There's a common trope that Berlin doesn't do customer service. However, while questions may be met with grunts at chain stores, the opposite is true at indie boutiques, helmed by friendly staff.

Shops tend to open from 10am to 8pm, but most are shut on Sunday. Still, Sunday flea markets offer a special kind of retail therapy in their place. Haggling is accepted, but asking for a plastic bag at any till isn't, so carry a tote bag.

ARTS & CULTURE

There are a handful of free museums and galleries in Berlin, but most change around €8–12 – it's these places that it's worth booking ahead for (they're rightly popular). Got tickets to the philharmonic or theatre? Smart casual is the way to go – just swerve the trainers you wore to Berghain last weekend.

NIGHTLIFE

Berliners don't rush their nights out – with weekend-long parties, there's no need to. Most clubs open at midnight on Friday and Saturday, but nobody turns up then; instead, people get together for dinner and drinks, then head to a club at 3am. Better yet, getting some sleep and going after breakfast is a Sunday ritual.

There's no silver bullet for hacking Berlin's notoriously tricky door policy, but some basics apply: know the name of the night and who's playing (the bouncer may quiz you), don't arrive drunk and dress down. That doesn't always mean black – some spots encourage colour, so do your research.

OUTDOORS

On sunny days, Berliners flock to the parks and waterways for gatherings and picnics. If you're BBQing in a park, only do so in a designated area called a *Grillplätze*, and take all your rubbish with you. You may be approached by a *Pfandsammler* (deposit collector) – often homeless folk who collect empties for the recycling deposit on each bottle.

Keep in mind

Here are some more tips and tidbits that will help you fit in like a local.

» **Cash is king** Many places still don't accept card, so keep enough cash on you.

» **No smoking** There's a ban on smoking inside, but many bars flout this or are *Raucherkneipen* (smokers' bars). Check ahead to ensure a bar is smoke-free.

» **Tipping** It's polite to tip waiters (10 per cent) and baristas (to the nearest euro), but it's not obligatory.

» **Stay hydrated** Thanks to the Refill Berlin initiative, many shops, bars and cafés will fill your water bottle for free – just look for a refill sticker and ask nicely.

GETTING AROUND

Once famously divided into East and West, Berlin is now split only by the River Spree, which runs through its heart. It's an enormous city, made up of 12 *Bezirke* (boroughs or districts, *p14*) that are further split into several *Kieze* (sub-districts). The famous sights you'll be most familiar with exist within the Ringbahn (or the Ring), a circular S-Bahn line that encloses the centre.

To make your life easy, we've provided what3words addresses for each sight in this book, meaning you can quickly pinpoint exactly where you're heading straight away.

On foot

In a city as pedestrian-friendly as Berlin, walking is the best way to get a feel for each *Kiez*. But, if we're honest, it's unrealistic to wander hood to hood – this is one of Europe's largest cities, after all. Instead, most locals head to their chosen *Kiez* by bike or with public transport (we'll come to that) and then embark on a walk around the area.

Nobody's ever in much of a hurry, so strolling takes a leisurely pace. That said, if you need to stop and check a what3words location, step to the side of the pavement. Jaywalking is sacrilegious and sometimes provokes an audible tut – especially if kids are around – so wait for the Ampelmann to go green when you're crossing the road.

On wheels

You'll struggle to find a Berliner who doesn't own a bike. Why? Well, cycling here is a breeze: it's mainly flat and there are over 660 km (410 miles) of bike lanes. Plus, if you get tired of pedalling, you can take your wheels on the U-Bahn, S-Bahn and trams – though you'll need to buy a bicycle ticket to do so.

It pays to be vigilant. Helmets aren't required, but this is the only time we'll advise you not to follow the locals – definitely wear one. Don't skip lights, watch out for cars turning right and be careful on roads with tram tracks, as it's easy to get your wheels stuck. If you're out after dark, ensure you have working lights and don't ride under the influence – having a blood alcohol level above 1.6 (the equivalent of two or three beers) could cost you your driver's licence.

Bike-sharing schemes are a saviour for visitors. Nextbike is the top provider, with tons of docking stations around town. Renting one will set you back €1 per 30 minutes or €15 for the week, and you simply leave it anywhere within the Ring for a 50c fee when you're done. *www.nextbike.de*

By public transport

Berlin's transport network is a well-oiled machine of 24/7 trains, buses and trams. There are three fare zones: A and B are within the city limits, and C covers parts of surrounding Brandenburg. The easiest way to buy a ticket is on the BVG app; if you opt for a paper ticket, you'll need to validate it at a time-stamping machine.

Barrier-free underground (U-Bahn) and commuter train (S-Bahn) stations make it tempting to dodge the fare; some choose to risk the €60 fine but inspectors are common, so don't try it.

You'll most likely encounter the Berliner *Schnauze*, a gruff attitude like New Yorkers' grittiness, on transport – don't be offended if people are curt or barge past, they're softies really. This goes both ways, so you don't have to apologize for every brushed shoulder.

By car or taxi

Roughly a third of Berliners own cars, though it's less likely the more centrally you live. If you do need to drive, opt for a car-sharing firm like DriveNow.

Registered taxis are reasonable, safe and bookable via Free Now – they're usually reserved for airport runs, late-night trips or the post-club exodus.
www.drivenow.com
www.free-now.com

Download these

We recommend you download these apps to help you get about the city.

WHAT3WORDS

A what3words address is a simple way to communicate any precise location on earth, using just three words. ///helpless.piston.same, for example, is the code for the *Fraternal Kiss* mural at the Berlin Wall. Simply download the free what3words app, type a what3words address into the search bar, and you'll know exactly where to go.

BVG FAHRINFO

Bar the S-Bahn, all public transport within Berlin is operated by the Berliner Verkehrsbetriebe (BVG). The official app is a one-stop shop for navigating the city, getting live updates, and working out the fastest route from A to B via transport planners and maps. You can also buy tickets via the app.

Berlin is a jigsaw of districts made up of Kieze *(micro-neighbourhoods), each with a distinct style and attitude. Here we take a look at some of our favourites.*

Berlin
NEIGHBOURHOODS

Charlottenburg

The only district that didn't touch the wall, Charlottenburg feels worlds away from the rest of uber-edgy Berlin. Highbrow culture, upscale spending and preserved old-world buildings (Schloss Charlottenburg, to name just one) have long attracted affluent elites to this part of the city. Yet, despite being home to the most exclusive shopping boulevard, Ku'Damm, it's not all sophisticated opulence. In down-to-earth **Wilmersdorf** to the south, leafy parks, cute cafés and quiet streets tempt families to put down roots. *{map 5}*

Friedrichshain

If any district epitomizes Berlin's alternative spirit, it's Friedrichshain. Punk allegiance lives on in dingy pubs, off-beat cinemas and lively alternative clubs – including hallowed ground Berghain. It's no wonder students make it their mission to live in the large shared apartments (known as WGs) in eastern **Samariterkiez**. But this isn't to say that Friedrichshain is all edge – dissident culture has been driven out by gentrifying forces since the wall fell. Once a hotbed for squatters, southeastern **Boxhagener Kiez** has seen the most changes, with new shops and restaurants forcing rents to rise. That said, the *Kiez* is still loved for its popular flea market and organic food shops: the domain of yuppies come the weekend. *{map 2}*

Kreuzberg

One of West Berlin's poorest districts during the Cold War, Kreuzberg has been through a huge glow-up since. It's trendy, buzzy and multicultural, home to the largest Turkish community outside of Turkey. Nowhere is this more true than in **Wrangelkiez** to the east, where busy bars and some of Berlin's best Turkish food (naturally) draw foodies in their droves. Things get more relaxed as you head south: in **Graefekiez**, youngsters hit up ethical fashion stores and co-working cafés, while mature Berliners call neighbouring **Bergmannkiez**, with its grand 19th-century buildings and wine shops, home. *{map 4}*

Mitte

It may be the city's busy tourist centre, dominated by selfie sticks at the likes of Checkpoint Charlie and Museumsinsel, but locals do still live in Mitte – albeit the high-earning kind. Plus, it's central (Mitte literally means "middle") and everyone has a reason to pop by, weaving through crowds to run errands or travelling through the city. And despite Mitte's hectic energy, there's peace and quiet to be found in the west, where an old Berlin feel pervades the leafy, residential area of **Moabit** – it's here that you'll find one of the longest-running market halls. {map 1}

Neukölln

Battling it out with neighbouring Kreuzberg for the title of hipster HQ, Neukölln is ground zero for young creatives. Despite being one of the city's fastest-gentrifying districts, rents remain cheap, and a multicultural, working-class make-up lives on. Take **Reuterkiez** to the north, where authentic restaurants thrive along "Arab Street" and artisan workshops draw in expats. A mere hop away in southern **Schillerkiez**, students enjoy a similar blend of old and new, with refurbished *Kneipen* (traditional Berlin beer bars) and a festival-like atmosphere in airfield-turned-park Tempelhof. {map 3}

Prenzlauer Berg

P-Berg, as it's lovingly known, is to the east what Charlottenburg is to the west: a pretty exclusive place to live. Nestled at the southern end of the large borough of Pankow, P-Berg may be bougie, but don't be fooled: as the story tends to go, this was once a squatters' paradise. Today, it's less edgy and more genteel, thanks to leafy parks, farmers' markets and boutiques – the majority of which lie in slick **Kollwitzkiez** to the south, where you can hardly move for prams and dogs. {map 1}

Schöneberg

An LGBTQ+ epicentre since the 1920s and an artist's paradise in the 1980s (this was where David Bowie lived out his Berlin years), this low-key district has long been a magnet for liberals. The crux of the LGBTQ+ scene plays out in **Winterfeldtplatz** in the north, where rainbow flags fly proudly in bookstores and restaurants, and colourful nightlife is a given. During the day, adjoining **Akanienkiez** buzzes with friends catching up in cute coffee shops before hitting up modern art galleries. {map 5}

Wedding

This northern district has been touted as Berlin's most "up-and-coming" area for years and, sure, a few brewpubs and restaurants keep the dream alive, but it's remained largely untouched by gentrifying forces. As a result, it continues to be pretty rough around the edges, leaving it much quieter than your Kreuzbergs or Neuköllns (aka, no queues for brunch). This laidback vibe is best felt in **Sprengelkiez**, where everyone seems to know each other and days pass socializing by the canal with beers. Dreamy. {map 6}

Berlin
ON THE MAP

Whether you're looking for your new favourite spot or want to check out what each part of Berlin has to offer, our maps – along with handy map references throughout the book – have you covered.

6

HENNIGSDORF

HEILIGENSEE

FALKENSEE

HAKENFELDE

B5

SPANDAU

A10

Grunewald

Spree

KLADOW

Havel

A115

NIKOLASSEE

Zernsee

POTSDAM

BABELSBERG

STAHNSDORF

WERDER

A10

A2

Schwielowsee

A115

0 kilometres   5

0 miles   5

MICHENDORF

A10

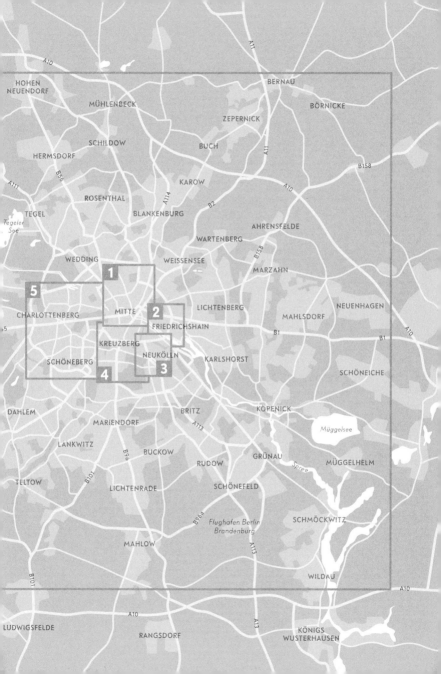

E Curry Baude

GLEIMVIERTEL

BEHMSTRASSE

SCHIVELBEINER STRASSE

WICHERTSTR.

STARGARDERSTR.

D Becketts Kopf

O Volkspark Humboldthain

GLEIMSTRASSE

BRUNNENVIERTEL

Mauerpark **S**

VINETA-PLATZ

VEB Orange **S**

E Kochu Karu

Prater Garten **D**

A Kulturbrauerei

E Street Food auf Achse

OYE Records **S**

ARKONA-PLATZ

Café Morgenrot **E**

Café Anna Blume

Saint George's

Berlin Wall Memorial **A**

Melting Point **S**

A Museum für Naturkunde

Buck & Breck **D**

E Black Isle

D 8MM Bar

N Spätkauf Rosenback

E Frea

KW Institute for Contemporary Art **A**

Clärchens Ballhaus **A**

Cuore di Vetro **S**

S Pro qm

House of Small Wonder **E**

N Babylon

Night Kitchen Berlin **E**

Ben Rahim **D**

S Made in Berlin

Sammlung Boros **A**

Kino Central **N A**

E Good Bank

Haus Schwarzenberg Complex

Monbijou-Ufer **N**

ALEXANDER-PLATZ

PLATZ DER REPUBLIK

Pergamon Museum **A**

Beate Uwe **N**

Maxim Gorki **A**

Neues Museum **A**

MUSEUMS-INSEL

Dussmann das KulturKaufhaus **S D**

Freundschaft

MITTE

Cookies Cream **E**

Staatsoper Unter den Linden **A**

N Porceptual

UNTER DEN LINDEN

FRANZÖSISCHE STRASSE

GENDARMEN-MARKT

FISCHER-INSEL

A Hošek Contemporary

0 metres   750

0 yards   750

LEIPZIGER STRASSE

SPITTEL-MARKT

MAP 1

0 metres 500
0 yards 500

LANDSBERGER ALLEE

FRIEDENSTRASSE

PALISADENSTRASSE

Kirchhof der St. Petri - Luisenstadtgemeinde

RICHARD-SORGE-STRASSE

PETERSBURGER STRASSE

THAERSTRASSE

STRAUSBERGER PLATZ

KARL-MARX-ALLEE

WEIDENWEG

BERSARIN-PLATZ

RIGAER STRASSE

Computerspielemuseum **A** **D** Briefmarken Weine

ANDREASSTRASSE

KOPPENSTRASSE

KARL-MARX-ALLEE

STRASSE DER PARISER KOMMUNE

FRIEDRICHSHAIN

RÜDERSDORFER STRASSE

Shakespeare and Sons **S**

GUBENER STRASSE

Protokoll **D** Zeroliq

D Kaffeehaus KuchenRausc

N Holzmarkt

Berghain **N**

HHV **S**

WARSCHAUER STRASSE

Boxhagener Platz

WÜHLISCHSTRASSE

Schilling-brücke

N Yaam

MÜHLENSTRASSE

Spree

Bis Aufs Messer **S**

Urban Spree **A**

Chantals House **N** of Shame

RAW Gelände

MODERSOHNSTRASSE

KÖPENICKER STRASSE

East Side **A** Gallery

Michelberger **D**

Monster Ronson's **N** Ichiban Karaoke

Folkdays **S**

WRANGELSTRASSE

Oberbaum-brücke

RUDOLFKIEZ

Markthalle Neun **E**

KREUZBERG

LAUSITZER PLATZ

Duo **E**

Bi Nuu **N**

E Burgermeister

STRALAUER ALLEE

SKALITZER STR.

S Motto Berlin

D Myśliwska

Spree

Quicky Markt **E** **N** Späti & Bar

N Madame Claude

SCHLESISCHE STR.

Kumpel & Keule Speisewirtschaft

GÖRLITZER

Café Mugrabi **E**

Stand-Up Paddleboarding on the Spree River **O** **O** Badeschiff

WIENER STRASSE

STRASSE

Club der **N** Visionaere

N MS Hoppetosse

Filmkunstbar **D** Fitzcarraldo

E Görlitzer Park

Landwehrkanal

S Arena

E Mama Shabz

Dingsdums Dumplings

Schlesischer Busch

ALT-TREPTOW

MAP 2

MAP 3

MAP 4

KitKat Club

Ohm

Spree

4

ORANIENSTRASSE

KOTTBUSSER TOR

KOTTBUSSER DAMM

HASENHEIDE

Volkspark
Hasenheide

Sommerbad
Neukölln

Allmende
Kontor

Ⓔ EAT

Kreuzberger Himmel *(p44)*
Mr. Minsch *(p49)*
Nobelhart & Schmutzig *(p38)*
Rocket + Basil *(p32)*

Ⓓ DRINK

BRLO Brwhouse *(p64)*
Golgatha *(p66)*
Westberlin *(p73)*

Ⓢ SHOP

Another Country *(p104)*
Die Espressionisten *(p103)*
Hallesches Haus *(p102)*
Trödelmarkt Marheinekeplatz *(p93)*
Vielfach *(p102)*

Ⓐ ARTS & CULTURE

Berliner Philharmoniker *(p126)*
F40 *(p125)*
Gropius Bau *(p120)*
HAU *(p127)*
Jüdisches Museum *(p123)*
KÖNIG GALERIE *(p118)*
Refugee Voice Tours *(p112)*
Tempodrom *(p124)*

Ⓝ NIGHTLIFE

Amici Amici Focacceria *(p141)*
Curry 36 *(p140)*
KitKat Club *(p147)*
Ohm *(p146)*
Sputnik *(p161)*
Zur Klappe *(p144)*

Ⓞ OUTDOORS

Allmende Kontor *(p175)*
Beach Volleyball at
   Beach Park 61 *(p183)*
Gemeinschaftsgarten Neue
   Grünstrasse *(p175)*
Park am Gleisdreieck *(p168)*
Prinzessinnengärten *(p173)*
Sommerbad Kreuzberg *(p177)*
Sommerbad Neukölln *(p176)*
Tempelhofer Feld *(p169)*
Viktoriapark *(p171)*

MAP 5

Erika Hess
Eisstadion

5

Fritz-
chloss-
Park

Hamburger
Bahnhof

Haus der
Kulturen
der Welt

Spree

STRASSE DES 17. JUNI

Tiergarten

KEMPER-
PLATZ

Schwules
Museum

POTSDAMER STRASSE

YORCKSTR

Neues Ufer

KOLONNENSTRASSE

🄴 EAT

893 Ryōtei *(p43)*
Arminiusmarkthalle *(p52)*
Bonvivant *(p39)*
Jones Ice Cream *(p51)*
Konditorei Buchwald *(p51)*
Lon Men's Noodle House *(p47)*
Madame Ngo *(p47)*
Malafemmena *(p45)*
Osmans Töchter *(p43)*
Son Kitchen *(p53)*

🄳 DRINK

Café am Neuen See *(p65)*
Café im Literaurhaus *(p74)*
CapRivi *(p67)*
Green Door *(p63)*
Möve im Felsenkeller *(p68)*
Rum Trader *(p60)*
Schleusenkrug *(p67)*
Schwarzes Café *(p79)*

🅂 SHOP

Bikini Berlin *(p100)*
Eisenherz *(p106)*
Manufactum *(p101)*
Markt am Winterfeldtplatz *(p95)*
Stilwerk *(p101)*
Strasse des 17. Juni *(p94)*

🄰 ARTS & CULTURE

Bauhaus-Archiv *(p112)*
Buchstabenmuseum *(p114)*
Hamburger Banhof *(p118)*
Haus der Kulturen der Welt *(p133)*
Museum für Fotografie *(p123)*
Schaubühne *(p125)*
Schwules Museum *(p113)*
Urban Nation *(p130)*
ZK/U *(p135)*

🄽 NIGHTLIFE

Astor Filmlounge *(p163)*
The Hat *(p151)*
Neues Ufer *(p152)*
Zig Zag *(p149)*

🄾 OUTDOORS

Erika Hess Eisstadion *(p180)*
Tiergarten *(p170)*

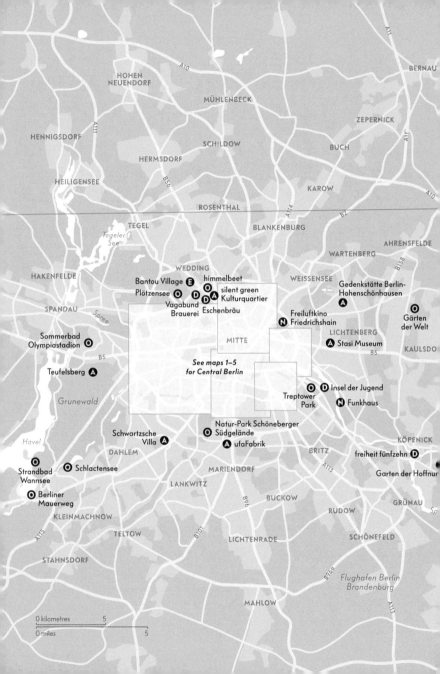

MAP 6

EAT

*As the German saying attests,
"Love goes through the stomach."
Cue Berlin's vibrant food scene,
which brings decades-old recipes
and bold new concepts together.*

Brunch Spots

Brunching is a sacred social ritual in Berlin – serious fortification for an afternoon of gallery hopping or a rite of recovery from yesterevening's antics. And in true Berlin style, offerings are anything but ordinary.

ROCKET + BASIL

Map 4; Lützowstrasse 22, Schöneberg; ///sleeping.steroids.coveted; www.rocketandbasil.com

Brunch is the ultimate self-care act at Rocket + Basil. The pretty café is run by German-Iranian sisters, whose fresh menu is inspired by their Persian heritage – think pistachio rosewater cake and healing herb broth. A bright space and laidback crowd, fresh from their midday yoga sessions, inspire a Zen state of mind, even during the lunch rush.

CAFÉ MORGENROT

Map 1; Kastanienallee 85, Prenzlauer Berg; ///crowds.rooftop.tiptoes; www.morgenrot.blogsport.eu

After the wall fell, Prenzlauer Berg was the epicentre of the left-alternative lifestyle. One place that still retains that spirit, despite gentrification in the area, is Café Morgenrot. Everything here is a beacon for positive change: the café is collectively organized, the food is always vegan or veggie, and many prices are based on a "pay what you can" concept. Every weekend, activists settle beside young families, all hoping to invoke change over brunch. Arrive early – it's only open 11am–3pm. Besides, revolutionary discussions take their time.

CAFÉ ANNA BLUME

Map 1; Kollwitzstrasse 83, Kollwitzkiez, Prenzlauer Berg;
///troubles.sang.space; www.cafe-anna-blume.de

We have this place to thank for kicking off Berlin's brunch craze back in 2005. Despite the influx of your typical "avo on toast" spots since, Café Anna Blume has stayed true to its roots, serving traditional German breakfast to P-Berg families and out-of-towners (often escorted by their German hosts) willing to queue on weekends. They all come for the tiered breakfast tray of meat, cheeses and scrambled eggs.

» Don't leave without visiting the adjoining flower shop after your meal, where vibrant bouquets and heavenly scents await.

HOUSE OF SMALL WONDER

Map 1; Auguststrasse 11–3, Mitte; ///ribs.insect.cultivation;
www.houseofsmallwonder.de

Following in the footsteps of its Brooklyn sister, this café has a loyal fan base among its chic Mitte regulars. Yes, the greenhouse vibes look great on their social feeds, but the menu has them replacing phones with forks. Here, tasty egg-centric dishes are inspired by *yōshoku* – a Japanese-American fusion cuisine – like the fabled Okinawan taco rice and biscuit Benedict.

Liked by the locals

"Growing up, I had no
comprehension of how
inspirational my mother and
aunties' cooking would be for me.
The café is a tribute to them and
my home. Because, let's be honest:
there's just no place like home."

SHABZ SAYED,
OWNER OF MAMA SHABZ

MAMA SHABZ

Map 2; Reichenberger Strasse 61, Kreuzberg; ///guardian.skills.merit;
www.mamashabz.com

Feeling homesick for the spicy aromatic flavours she grew up with,
Shabz Sayed – a Londoner of Kashmiri and Punjabi heritage –
decided to do something about it. Enter this Pakistani café, where
Shabz cooks heartwarming dishes (dals, pakoras, curries) inspired
by family recipes. Come on Saturday, when brunch is served thali-style.
» Don't leave without buying some jarred goods from the café store,
like a Masala Chai spice mix, to make your own tasty brunch at home.

GEIST IM GLAS

Map 3; Lenaustrasse 27, Neukölln; ///printing.composed.ruled;
www.geistimglas.de

Okay, maybe there's no official cure for a hangover, but the
weekend brunch here might just be the closest thing. *Dulce de leche*
pancakes, fried chicken waffles, Bloody Marys and bottomless filter
coffee will have you up for more Berlin high jinks in no time.

CAFÉ MUGRABI

Map 2; Görlitzer Strasse 58, Kreuzberg; ///twig.retina.sentences;
www.en.cafemugrabi.com

Low-key, bona fide brunches are few and far between in Berlin, which
is why this outdoor spot overlooking Görlitzer Park is such a hit. After-
party vibes prevail in the summer, when fans trickle in post clubbing
for generous portions of Israeli specialities. Shakshuka, anyone?

Sustainable Dining

Sustainability isn't a trend in Berlin – it's a lifestyle. Going organic borders on an obsession, nose-to-tail spots satisfy those who haven't gone vegan (very few) and zero-waste is no fantasy. Other cities, take note.

KUMPEL & KEULE SPEISEWIRTSCHAFT

Map 2; Skalitzer Strasse 97, Kreuzberg; ///recall.brightly.unfolds; www.kumpelundkeule.de

Ask any carnivore where you'll find the city's most tasty, tender cuts and they'll point you towards this nose-to-tail joint. All the meat is sourced from regional German farmers and sliced and diced by the cool, tattooed butchers at the Kumpel & Keule butchery in nearby Markthalle Neun *(p53)*. The result is a hearty

Try it!
MAKE THE CUT

Fancy whipping up your own ethical meal? Check out the events at sustainable café Hermann's *(www.hermanns.com)*, where you might learn how the vegan sausage is made or how to bake sourdough bread.

German-inspired menu of dry-aged steaks, free-range chicken and fresh handmade sausages – the kind that put all the production-line wursts around Berlin to shame.

NEUE REPUBLIK REGER

Map 3; Bouchéstrasse 79A, Alt-Treptow; ///fanfare.fits.sobered; www.republik.sexy

It's not often people draw on their uni thesis post graduation, but one of the owners here had an idea worth sharing: the "ideal nation". Thanks to a crowdfunding initiative, the New Republic Reger has aimed to be just that, sourcing ingredients from organic farmers and donating to social projects (pretty ideal). The manifesto? You can't change the world on an empty stomach, so order some vegan fast food treats (the poutine is unreal) and get ready to fight the system.

» Don't leave without ordering a REPUBLIK EXPORT BEER – €1 goes to Bikeygees eV, a cycling training initiative for refugee women.

FREA

Map 1; Torstrasse 180, Mitte; ///miles.grabs.engages; www.frea.de

The world's first zero-waste vegan restaurant lacks for nothing. Rotating dishes fashioned from local farm produce? Check. Think homemade dips with fresh sourdough and veggie terrine. A good conscience? Try a great one: anything you don't eat is composted and returned to suppliers. A chic eco haven to enjoy it in? Naturally: those lamps set up beside you are made from mushroom fibre, and that chair you're sitting on is upcycled.

GOOD BANK

Map 1; Rosa-Luxemburg-Strasse 5, Mitte; ///observer.tolls.rungs;
www.shop.good-bank.de

This futuristic, innovative spot could hardly be more Berlin. At the
world's first vertical farm-to-table restaurant, the veggies for the
salads and soups on the menu are grown and harvested behind
the counters, meaning less transportation and packaging waste.
The meat is sourced from farms committed to animal welfare,
too, should you opt for a beef sandwich for lunch instead.

ATAYACAFFE

Map 1; Zelterstrasse 6, Prenzlauer Berg; ///breezes.divider.flip;
www.atayacaffe.de

Born from the love story of a couple from Sardinia and Senegal,
this African-Italian vegan spot connects food with happiness and
healing. Ataya's cheery regulars, snuggled up on a sofa while tucking
into jollof rice bowls and handmade pastas (all prepared with zero-
waste, plastic-free sensibility), are a testament to this vision.

NOBELHART & SCHMUTZIG

Map 4; Friedrichstrasse 218, Mitte; ///clinked.blocks.used;
www.nobelhartundschmutzig.com

"Brutally local" is the name of the game here – yes, the literal game
served up. Kick-starting Berlin's sustainable food movement, this
fine dining spot was the first to seek out and showcase regional
farmers; in short, if an ingredient – from the meat down to the

salt – can't be produced in Berlin or its surrounds, it won't be used. Each seasonal dish (part of a fixed ten-course menu) is served with a story, too, so you'll leave feeling like you know the hunter behind that deer rump or farmer who harvested that kohlrabi. Yes, it's spenny, and phones are banned, but a visit here is truly one of a kind.

BONVIVANT

Map 5; Goltzstrasse 32, Schöneberg; ///homework.tulip.trams; www.bonvivant.berlin

This place is based around a unique concept: Germany's first vegetarian cocktail bistro, where the drinks are just as sustainable as the food. And these aren't just any cocktails; they're made with fresh herbs from Bonvivant's own garden. This, matched with chef Ottmar Pohl-Hoffbauer's seasonal vegetarian tapas (he adapts his menu based on the crop plans of regional farmers), quickly won fans.

» Don't leave without trying a signature cocktail. Some arrive with a scented element, so the bartender may spray something on your hand.

DINGSDUMS DUMPLINGS

Map 2; Wiener Strasse 34, Kreuzberg; ///shuttle.funds.extreme; www.dingsdums.de

Green cuisine can come with a hefty price tag, so all hail DD owners Mau and Anna, who quit their day jobs to make sustainable eating mainstream (read: make it street food) and affordable. How? They buy in surplus "flawed" items that would've been thrown out and deep fry them in colourful dough. Zero-waste, but make it hip.

Special Occasion

Finally got that start-up off the ground? Entering a new decade of birthdays? Berlin's got every celebration covered, with boundary-pushing and inventive spots that embody the city's creative spirit and rebel heart.

NIGHT KITCHEN BERLIN

Map 1; Oranienburger Strasse 32, Heckmann Höfe, Mitte;
///saunas.sugar.tailing; www.nightkitchenberlin.com

Welcome to the most vibrant Tel Aviv dinner party – your host, a boisterous Israeli, has already poured shots and served hummus before you've barely taken off your winter parka. Night Kitchen is that sort of place: warm Mediterranean vibes in a classy hidden courtyard that feels very Isherwood. Come for a laidback dinner with visiting friends and feast on the family-style sharing plates.

KOCHU KARU

Map 1; Eberswalder Strasse 35, Prenzlauer Berg;
///scoot.balance.vitals; www.kochukaru.de

This is the kind of neighbourhood joint that everyone wants at the end of their road. The menu blends Asian and Mediterranean flavours, the interior resembles an upscale tapas bar and the

Some nights, trained soprano Bini sings opera while you eat. Check the website and book accordingly. | service is as friendly as you'll get. Add to that the odd live performance, and there's nowhere better for a no-fuss birthday bash.

COOKIES CREAM

Map 1; Behrenstrasse 55, Westin Grand Hotel, Mitte; ///almost.litters.yards; www.cookiescream.com

This place holds legendary status – both as the first vegetarian spot to nab a Michelin star, and as a venue where dinners once preceded a night partying in the now defunct club downstairs. While former ravers recall those glory days as they wine and dine here, Cookies Cream looks firmly to the future, always reinventing itself with whimsical new dishes.

» Don't leave without ordering a dessert. The menu changes a lot and tends to be full of unique concoctions like apricots with saffron ice cream.

CODA

Map 3; Friedelstrasse 47, Reuterkiez, Neukölln; ///abode.tiny.quality; www.coda-berlin.com

Ever pondered what dinner could be if it was just desserts? Germany's first and only desserts restaurant is way ahead of you. Seven courses of otherworldly pastries paired with alcoholic drinks might sound heavy, but a sugar crash is not on the menu – nor is white sugar itself. Rather, sweetness is achieved through natural alchemy and intensive techniques like fermentation. Who needs a birthday cake?

Liked by the locals

"The restaurant scene in Berlin is full of surprises – not only in terms of culinary diversity, but also with unusual locations. At Osmans Töchter, traditional Turkish dishes meet tasty new interpretations."

LALE YANIK, CO-OWNER OF
OSMANS TÖCHTER

LAVANDERIA VECCHIA

Map 3; Flughafenstrasse 46, Neukölln; ///cans.cheaply.pies;
www.lavanderiavecchia.wordpress.com

A restaurant in a former laundromat may not seem unusual in a city
where galleries take over former crematoriums, but what is surprising
is how romantic this spot is – washing lines and all. Rather than
arguing with your date over whose turn it is to change the sheets, you'll
be cooing over authentic Italian food by the flicker of candlelight.

893 RYŌTEI

Map 5; Kantstrasse 135–6, Charlottenburg;
///ripe.fencing.ports; www.893ryotei.de

Don't be fooled by the sketchy-looking exterior – this is a high-end
sushi joint. A visit is as much about the show as the meal, so book seats
along the open kitchen for thrilling views of grilling and sashimi-slicing.
» Don't leave without starting the night off with a sake martini – the
perfect drink to toast that promotion or new job.

OSMANS TÖCHTER

Map 5; Wielandstrasse 38, Charlottenburg; ///horses.thank.sardine;
www.osmanstoechterberlin.de

Growing up, Turkish-German owners Arzu and Lale realized just how
much the preparing of Turkish dishes brought their family and friends
together – and Osman's Daughters encourages the same. It feels
like dining at your mum's house, with families nattering at the tables
and chefs dishing up beloved childhood recipes from the open kitchen.

Global Grub

Berlin's brightly multicultural, highly immigrant make-up is good fortune for the foodie scene. Dining here is a globetrotting endeavour, whether you're gorging in a Turkish stalwart or an Italian kitchen.

KREUZBERGER HIMMEL

Map 4; Yorckstrasse 89, Kreuzberg; ///napkins.scraper.bucked; www.kreuzberger-himmel.de

When tens of thousands of newcomers arrived in Berlin during the 2015 refugee crisis, journalist Andreas Tölke set out to create a homely space to welcome them. Two years later Kreuzberg Heaven – a restaurant that only employs refugees – was born. Everything about this place builds community: grandparents share sought-after tables

Try it!
FIND REFUGE

Want to expand your recipe book and make pals while doing so? Refugee Dinners *(www.refugeedinners.org)* offers cooking classes taught by refugees in their homeland cuisine, all hosted in Berliners' homes.

with fashion students, bonding over authentic Syrian dishes, sitting on furniture donated by local artists and listening to stories from Syrian chefs and Pakistani waiters. Here, good food transcends barriers.

>> Don't leave without trying a white wine from Lebanon, whose ancient wine-producing regions are undergoing a renaissance.

MALAFEMMENA

Map 5; Hauptstrasse 85, Schöneberg; ///pipeline.smelter.clouds; www.malafemmena.restaurant

Debates on Berlin's best Neapolitan pizzeria are always lively, sometimes heated and never settled. Plus, with endless pizza joints popping up, the margins are thin. But we think this neighbourhood spot edges it. Why? Because it's the most authentic slice this side of Naples. Piping hot pies fly out of an original Forno Valoriani oven, all topped with produce imported from Italy and proudly served by outgoing Italian staff bustling between tables.

DOYUM

Map 3; Admiralstrasse 36–7, Kreuzberg; ///striving.daisy.risk; www.doyum-restaurant.de

Home to the largest Turkish community outside of Turkey, Berlin unsurprisingly brims with excellent Turkish restaurants. And Doyum tops the pile. Tiled walls, busy waiters and sweet charcoal aromas make you feel like you're dining by the Bosporus, not on a quiet corner of Kreuzberg. Then there's the food. Think hearty soups, homemade *lahmacun* and generous kebabs served straight from the grill.

Solo, Pair, Crowd

Craving an epic feast? Or want to heat up a date? There's a different cuisine for your every mood in Berlin.

FLYING SOLO
Belting breakfast
Stumped for morning plans? Pit stop at Kreuzberg's Leylak to pick up some Turkish *börek*. Arrive first thing to get these stuffed pastries fresh out the oven.

IN A PAIR
Spice it up
Dates don't get much more intimate than at Moabit's Agni. With only three tables inside, this tiny Indian kitchen does some of the best curry in Berlin.

FOR A CROWD
Come together
Tantalizing smells of Israeli and Palestinian fare hit you as soon as you enter Kanaan in Prenzlauer Berg. The sharing plates are perfect for groups searching for the "best hummus in town" – so the sign says outside.

MADAME NGO

Map 5; Kantstrasse 30, Charlottenburg; ///clubs.transmitted.talker;
www.madame-ngo.de

In a city where there seems to be a pho spot around every corner, you can count on Madame Ngo for the most flavourful bowl. Excellent-quality meat, a mystery spice blend (they'll never tell) and a huge vat of broth simmering for hours in the window is the reason why.

BANTOU VILLAGE

Map 6; Kameruner Strasse 2, Wedding; ///able.puppets.stove;
www.bantou-village-berlin.de

Stepping inside this warm Cameroonian restaurant is like being transported to Yaoundé: big groups of African diners drink beer and make merry, music videos blare from the flat-screen TV and generous portions of West African dishes abound. The service is a tad slow when the place is packed (always), but when you're making friends with the regulars at the table beside you, what's the rush?

LON MEN'S NOODLE HOUSE

Map 5; Kantstrasse 33, Charlottenburg; ///harvest.chefs.spirits

Everyone and their flatmate knows this Taiwanese noodle joint. It's one of those rare restaurants where, over the decades, the menu never changes, the prices don't seem to go up and the food comes out fast, delicious and smelling divine every time.

» Don't leave without trying the wonton in chilli oil – many declare that it's the best wonton dish in the city. We aren't arguing.

Sweet Treats

For all its gritty glory, Berlin has a sweet side too – or rather, a sweet tooth. Ice cream is devoured year-round (yep, even during arctic winters) and artisanal pastries with good coffee are weekend staples.

DUO

Map 2; Skalitzer Strasse 82, Kreuzberg; ///unzips.deprive.shorter; www.duoicecream.de

When family secrets and food combine, you're pretty much guaranteed something special. And that's exactly what you get at this much-loved gelato shop. Second-generation owner Antonio learned the art of churning from his father, a Sicilian who opened

Shh!

So you've heard of *Kaffee und Kuchen* (the afternoon coffee and cake tradition), but what about *Lördagsgodis*? Okay, it's not a German thing, but eating sweets on a Saturday is huge in Sweden – which is where Herr Nilsson GODIS *(www.herrnilsson. com)*, an underrated pick 'n' mix shop owned by a Swedish-German couple, comes in. Buy some salty liquorice and enjoy.

this parlour in 1972, and still uses his recipes today. People happily wait their turn outside, peeking through the door to see Antonio liberally scoop silky gelato into waffles and brioche buns.

MR. MINSCH

Map 4; Yorckstrasse 15, Kreuzberg; ///dusts.locked.tender;
www.mr-minsch-torten.de

Lazy Sunday strollers have a habit of meandering towards the massive queue outside this cake shop. Part of the joy is peeking through the large window to the open kitchen, where cheery bakers prepare 20 different cakes each day – everything from vegan apple walnut to classics like carrot cake, all displayed and sold by the (very generous) slice. When you've finally made your mind up, settle on a chair outside and prepare to get evangelical.

» Don't leave without trying a slice of the *Mohnstreuselkuchen*, a classic German poppy seed cake baked to perfection.

ALBATROSS

Map 3; Graefestrasse 66–7, Neukölln; ///dwelled.laser.ranch;
www.albatrossberlin.com

Though this trendy bakery is revered for its sourdough bread (boujie foodies swear by it), it's the flaky pastries that keep loyal fans returning. Come the weekend, cinnamon rolls, Danishes and stout little French *kouign amann* (a kind of caramelized croissant on steroids) are plucked into paper bags, providing well-heeled locals with winning treats to present at brunch round their mate's house.

CUORE DI VETRO

Map 1; Max-Beer-Strasse 33, Mitte; ///leotard.singers.kipper;
www.cuoredivetro.berlin

It may be called Heart of Glass in honour of Werner Herzog's film, but really, the name of this ice cream spot is a metaphor for its glass-walled kitchen, where 16 varieties of artisanal gelato are churned out daily. Once you've pulled your eyes off the handmade production process, it's decision time: pistachio, vegan chocolate sorbet, tiramisu gelato?

BLACK ISLE

Map 1; Weinbergsweg 23, Mitte; ///blurred.things.bits;
www.blackislebakery.com

If it wasn't for the delicious goodies, framed in a sleek cabinet, you'd mistake this place for another Mitte gallery. And that's the point. When Scot Ruth Barry quit her job in London's art world to pursue her love of baking, it made sense to bring the soul of a gallery to this space. White walls and burnished tabletops set the scene for masterpiece brownies, vegan banana breads and lemon drizzle cakes. Artfully done.

» Don't leave without trying a slice of the famous millionaire shortbread. The buttery caramel combo is the best of British in a bite.

LA MAISON

Map 3; Paul-Lincke-Ufer 17, Kreuzberg; ///restriction.plus.warbler

If you happen to pass a chic Berliner mid-canalside stroll, rest assured they're en route to this French patisserie for a little *je ne sais quoi*. As soon as the sun's out, the terrace fills up with laissez-faire locals, idling

If every seats is taken, grab a treat and watch some *pétanque* on the embankment outside. Blink and you're in Paris.

away their afternoons over golden *tartelettes* and strong coffee. Those who live for the simple crunch of buttery puff pastry should try the croissants; many consider them Berlin's finest.

KONDITOREI BUCHWALD

Map 5; Bartningallee 29, Moabit; ///shock.removes.remote;
www.konditorei-buchwald.de

Open since 1852, the city's oldest confectioner is steadfast in always-changing Berlin, still serving up a slice of traditional *Kaffee und Kuchen* culture. Family run for five generations, it's the only place any Berliner worth their pastry would come for a layered sponge *Baumkuchen* (the speciality cake here) and chocolatey Sachertorte. Its kitsch vibe may not be the coolest in town, but smiling regulars suggest nobody really cares – and who would when the cake is this good?

JONES ICE CREAM

Map 5; Goltzstrasse 3, Schöneberg; ///spurned.laws.monopoly;
www.jonesicecream.com

If forced to choose Berlin's best ice cream parlour, American expats would vote Jones. Yes, the decadent small-batch ice creams are to die for, but what sets Jones apart are the sweet treats: chewy fresh-baked cookies (on top of which ice cream gets shovelled) and homemade waffle cones. Heavenly smells are enough to draw lengthy queues, so arrive no later than 3pm before the cookies, at least, sell out.

Street Food

*Berlin eats on its feet. For every hip new restaurant opening there's a time-honoured snack kiosk (**Imbiss**) or casual food market serving up quick comfort food and unpretentious vibes.*

CURRY BAUDE

Map 1; Badstrasse 1–5, Wedding; ///vast.sour.soils; www.curry-baude.de

Though thousands of stalls sell *Currywurst*, the spicy sausage that is Berlin's pride and joy, this subway kiosk is where Berliners come for a Class A fix of secret sauces and family recipes. As you approach, the larger-than-life owner, a former butcher, barks "*mit oder ohne Darm?*" through a small window hatch. Don't stress: he's just asking whether you want your sausage with or without skin, a dealbreaker round these parts. Get it unpeeled – it's a Berlin creation.

ARMINIUSMARKTHALLE

Map 5; Arminiusstrasse 2–4, Moabit; ///evolving.every.soils;
www.arminiusmarkthalle.com

Flying well under the tourist radar, this gem of a market hall has held a place in local hearts since 1891. On Saturdays, grey-haired residents do their weekly produce shopping while a younger crew savour

Visiting Berlin in the summer? Soak up the vibes at Bite Club, the city's favourite pop-up street food and party series.

Peruvian ceviche and Alabama BBQ from food stalls. Greengrocers coexist with Canadian poutine vendors, and it works. It's still serving the community's needs, old and new, a century on, adding to its charm.

MARKTHALLE NEUN

Map 2; Eisenbahnstrasse 42–3, Kreuzberg; ///climber.along.glitz;
www.markthalleneun.de

After an organic vegan ice cream producer? On the hunt for a female tofu-making duo? This indoor market hall, a creative hub for Berlin's gastro scene, seems to feature every independent, sustainable foodie hero you could want. Since word got out about the famed Street Food Thursdays, locals prefer to hit up M9 on Saturday mornings, gossiping about the week over a smorgasbord of treats.

» Don't leave without stopping by Kumpel & Keule for a burger, assembled with ingredients from around the Markthalle. Pretty neat.

SON KITCHEN

Map 5; Kantstrasse 46, Charlottenburg; ///slamming.trees.legwork;
www.sonkitchen.de

This tiny red-tiled spot stands like a beacon among Kantstrasse's Asian joints. The owners, three lads with German and Korean roots, combine the best of both culinary cultures on their addictive menu. If the snack-sized bites flogged from a window are a nod to the *Imbiss*, the food – think kimchi tacos and *bibimbap* – is in a different league.

Liked by the locals

"The Turkish market is a way
for the local Turkish community
and immigrants to take part
in social life in Kreuzberg. It
enables Turks to live together
and secures their place in a
gentrifying neighbourhood."

MEHMET KÜÇÜK, GERMAN-TURKISH VIDEO PRODUCER

STREET FOOD AUF ACHSE

Map 1; Schönhauser Allee 38, Prenzlauer Berg; ///audibly.boat.mimics; www.streetfoodaufachse.de

Where food trucks go, Berliners follow – when this weekend market Street Food on the Move rolls around, at least. Tempting locals are wafting spices from Fräulein Kimchi and sizzling grills at Humble Pie (to name but a couple of trendy mainstays here).

» Don't leave without eating a traditional Roman Pinsa (a lighter, slightly healthier version of pizza) from San Pietrino Pinsa.

TÜRKISCHER MARKT

Map 3; Maybachufer, Neukölln; ///sailor.quality.sunshine

Walking through the bazaar-esque Turkish market is a sensory blitz: sizzling grills, vegetable sellers yelling out prices, Turkish grannies and high-fashion hipsters milling about. Though it's also open on Tuesday, Saturday is where it's at, when delightful chaos ensues as anyone and everyone gorges on Turkish, African and Thai bites.

BURGERMEISTER

Map 2; Oberbaumstrasse 8, Kreuzberg; ///safely.enforced.dating; www.burger-meister.de

Juicy patties have been flipped in this converted public loo for two decades – way before the burger craze swept the city. It still lives up to the wordplay in its name; it *is* the master, but it's also a mere umlaut away from being the mayor of all burger joints. Just ask the fans who huddle here for lunchtime pick-me-ups and late-night indulgences.

The Turkish kebab shop **Imren Grill** opened a little after the wall came down, and is still beloved by Neukölln's Arab community today.

KOTTBUSSER DAMM

MAYBACHUFER

HOHENSTAUFEN-PLATZ

PFLÜGERSTRASSE

LENAUSTRASSE

REUTERSTRASSE

Make friends at
SHAREHAUS REFUGIO CAFÉ

4

End with a flat white and homemade banana bread at this café, run entirely by live-in refugees. There may even be a workshop on.

Graze at
FALAFEL JAKOUB

REUTER-PLATZ

This falafel shop is a favourite – especially at night when hungry crowds line up. Order a falafel plate dripping in tahini to share, and you'll see what all the fuss is about.

3

HERMANN-PLATZ

Lunch at
ALDIMASHQI

2

Skip the takeaway crowd queuing out front and head inside. Unlike at a lot of Berlin kebab stations, the high-quality meat here is hand-cut from the skewer.

WESERSTRASSE

SONNENALLEE

HERMANNSTRASSE

Volkspark Hasenheide

KARL-MARX-STRASSE

NEUKÖLLN

FLUGHAFENSTRASSE

0 metres		300
0 yards		300

An afternoon of
Arab flavours

Boulevards don't get more dynamic than Sonnennallee, a 5-km- (3-mile-) long stretch in Neukölln, better known as "Arab Street". A Middle Eastern community has traded along this street since the 1970s, and it's really made waves in the last decade for its buzzing food scene. That's somewhat down to the area's Syrian immigrants, who fled the war in 2015 and set up businesses here, drawing on the culinary delights of their hometowns. Spend the afternoon grazing and soaking up the community spirit along this street.

Treat yourself at
KONDITOREI DAMASKUS
Pick up an assortment of baklava to enjoy later. The family at this spot's helm used to own a pastry shop in Syria, so you know it's the good stuff.

1. Konditorei Damaskus
Sonnenallee 93, Neukölln;
www.damaskus-konditorei-emissa.com
///stubble.gearbox.secures

2. Aldimashqi
Reuterstrasse 28, Neukölln;
0176 6106 5784
///contour.copes.acrobat

3. Falafel Jakoub
Weserstrasse 14, Neukölln;
www.falafeljakoub.
eatbu.com
///reboot.robots.settle

4. Sharehaus Refugio Café
Lenaustrasse 3–4, Neukölln;
www.refugio.berlin
///prosper.library.them

 Imren Grill ///staple.tailing.packet

DRINK

Beer gardens, bars and cafés are the lifeblood of Berlin, where time is spent project-planning over a strong espresso and bantering with a home-brewed beer in hand.

Secret Speakeasies

Nothing says Berlin like an underground drinking den. Harking back to the splendour of the 1920s (with a nod to the 2020s), speakeasies here promise sultry corners and strong drinks.

RUM TRADER

Map 5; Fasanenstrasse 40, Charlottenburg-Wilmersdorf; ///mashing.oiled.fall; (030) 881 1428

Not everyone loves Rum Trader, but therein lies its charm. The furniture is creaky, there are only around 10 seats and the gruff barman-owner – always donning a bow tie and pocket watch – will turn you away without blinking if you're with more than two mates. He works alone, and might take his spaghetti dinner break at the bar, so don't expect your rum cocktail to be made post-haste. Certainly one of a kind.

BUCK & BRECK

Map 1; Brunnenstrasse 177, Mitte; ///tempting.alas.shadows; www.buckandbreck.com

An exclusive speakeasy with a dash of Berlin punk – that's Buck & Breck. Behind a fake storage area, bartenders with baseball caps, coiffed beards and arm-sleeve tattoos make libations with a punch while couples murmur on barstools and chain-smoke next to quirky artwork. Go early – like, Berlin early – at 8pm, ring the buzzer labelled "BAR" and look discerning. No space? The bartender might take your number and call when a table is free (if he likes your vibe, that is).

» Don't leave without trying the signature Buck & Breck, a potent cocktail with champagne and cognac dating back to the 19th century.

BECKETTS KOPF

Map 1; Pappelallee 64, Prenzlauer Berg; ///dozen.nearing.employer; www.becketts-kopf.de

What started as a hobby in cocktail making for husband-and-wife duo Oliver and Cristina swiftly turned into this honest-to-goodness speakeasy. Former theatre director Oliver (the portrait of Samuel Beckett fronting this bar makes sense now, right?) learned everything he knows from scouring mixology books, and it's paid off. Let the bartender know what drink you're lusting after and it'll be shaken up.

BÜRKNER ECK

Map 3; Hobrechtstrasse 39, Neukölln; ///basher.filer.figs; www.buerknereck.simpleshop.com

The kind of welcoming bar that everyone should have on their block, Bürkner Eck is that friend's house you never want to leave. Whether dropping by for a pre-dinner bev or Saturday's 4am finale round, Neukölln expats hang loose in retro flannel and baggy jeans, sipping old-fashioneds and negronis on antique furniture. Wave by the door and wait to be buzzed in – see, just like your mate's house.

Liked by the locals

"Berlin has something wild in the water, so burlesque here makes sense. The 1920s cabaret scene has had a major impact on the burlesque we see in shows today. This city and striptease were made for each other."

LA VIOLA VIXEN, BURLESQUE DANCER AND DIRECTOR OF THE SHIMMY SHAKE BERLIN BURLESQUE SCHOOL

GREEN DOOR

Map 5; Winterfeldtstrasse 50, Schöneberg; ///tiny.graceful.gifts;
www.greendoor.de

During Prohibition, green doors marked the speakeasies where
illegal booze could be found, but thankfully, the bold front here is more
of a gimmick now. Ring the doorbell, order a famed champagne-
heavy Curtain Call and enjoy a great cocktail – legally.

TRUFFLE PIG

Map 3; Reuterstrasse 47, Neukölln; ///follow.dose.timeless; www.trufflepig.de

While regulars sink pints inside the Kauz & Kiebitz pub, a motley crowd
slink past them, following the pig tracks that lead to this hidden
speakeasy inside. If you're brave enough to follow suit and ring the
bell, you'll join DJs relaxing before a club night set and sophisticated
drinkers enjoying the perfect *Absacker* (nightcap).

PRINZIPAL

Map 3; Oranienstrasse 178, Kreuzberg; ///magnets.painting.levels;
www.prinzipal-kreuzberg.com

The Golden Twenties are alive and well at this chichi Weimar-
inspired spot. Glamorous patrons enter through an unmarked
green door, costumed mixologists embody old-world zazz in bow
ties and corsets, and burlesque dancers tease on a small stage
most weekends (when reservations are essential).

» Don't leave without being extra nice to the staff – they might let you
peek into the costume closet of feather headdresses and fringed getups.

Beer Gardens

*The **Biergarten** is a Berlin institution, built on the city's love for alfresco drinking – which gets all the more ceremonial in summer. It's about more than the beer, though, with cheerful vibes and an infectious buzz.*

PRATER GARTEN

Map 1; Kastanienallee 7–9, Prenzlauer Berg; ///elated.pots.fenced; www.prater-biergarten.de

Open any Berlin guide and you'll find this bustling joint topping the list of open-air watering holes – it's Berlin's oldest beer garden, after all. But don't assume it's a tourist hotspot. You're more likely to sit beside parched locals cooling down after a hard day's graft than camera-wielding selfie-takers. There's enough room for 600 punters, so you'll have your pick of the seats (should a selfie stick enter your sphere).

BRLO BRWHOUSE

Map 4; Schöneberger Strasse 16, Gleisdreieck Park, Kreuzberg; ///braced.fines.being; www.brlo-brwhouse.de

It's a typical story around these parts: three beer-loving college pals found a craft beer brand, Berliners go crazy for it, said brand opens a beer garden selling their brews, and a state of nirvana is reached.

If you're visiting in winter, check out the Christmas market here with *Glühwein* (mulled wine) and sausage-grilling.

That's exactly what happened with BRLO. Made entirely out of shipping containers, this terrace is the domain of skateboarders, who lounge on beach chairs with IPAs after a sesh in the adjoining park.

CAFÉ AM NEUEN SEE

Map 5; Lichtensteinallee 2, Tiergarten; ///detection.doted.dealings; www.cafeamneuensee.de

Rest assured that if it's sunny, you'll be fighting for a table at this idyllic den. Tucked within Tiergarten *(p170)* and beside a little lake, Café am Neuen See feels far from city life, its picnic tables scattered beneath leafy shade. If the fight for a table is lost, spread out on the grass with a date and swap life stories over dreamy views.

» Don't leave without renting a rowing boat on the itsy-bitsy lake and snapping some photos of the lush greenery. Perfect date, if you ask us.

INSEL DER JUGEND

Map 6; Insel der Jugend, Alt-Treptow; ///deflection.crouch.noises; www.inselberlin.de

Don't be deterred by the name – you needn't be fresh-faced to drink at the Island of Youth. Rather, it's all about forgetting the woes of adulthood over a pint of fresh Czech Pilsner straight from the tank. Cross the castle-like footbridge, settle into a deckchair and enjoy the sweeping views of the Spree, the surrounding woodland and the setting sun (trust us, you'll want to stay here till sunset).

GOLGATHA

Map 4; Katzbachstrasse, Kreuzberg; ///creamed.clearing.circular;
www.golgatha-berlin.de

When locals amble through Viktoriapark *(p171)*, they have one end point in mind: this little beer garden, nestled in a quiet corner. The name, a nod to the park's hilltop biblical cross, seems fitting given that outdoor drinking is a summertime ritual here. By day, families catch up beside the old Art Deco pavilion while kids play; come evening, a younger crew make a beeline for the benches up on the pavilion's roof (the best seats, we say), drinking well into those sultry summer nights.

FREIHEIT FÜNFZEHN

Map 6; Freiheit 15, Köpenick; ///suspend.digress.shot; www.freiheit15.com

Köpenick might not be the first area on everyone's list of places to see (third-wave coffee shops are starkly absent, renowned superclubs are nowhere to be found and don't even bother looking for artisanal bread). Yet, it's one of the few places that locals are willing to schlep

An old gymnasium may not be the most obvious choice for a cold pint (flashbacks to school PE lessons included), but that's exactly why Alte Turnhalle *(www.dieturnhalle.de)* remains a well-kept secret. A quaint little beer garden is attached to this events venue in Friedrichshain, where leather couches are dotted around palm trees, and relaxation is the only order.

to. That's all down to its scenic beer garden: backed by a majestic castle, surrounded by water and with views out to Baumgarteninsel. (Whisper about this place in hushed tones, please.)

CAPRIVI

Map 5; Am Spreebord, Charlottenburg; ///define.audibly.atoms;
www.caprivi-berlin.com

If guidebooks tell you that Schloss Charlottenburg is a must-see when in Berlin, then locals will say that popping by this nearby riverside spot after a palace mooch is even more essential. After-work folk sinking a pint own the night here, so if the benches are full, take your tipple to the embankment and see how many tourists you can get to wave from the passing riverboats.

» Don't leave without watching the sunset from the nearby Siemenssteg, a handsome old footbridge spanning the Spree.

SCHLEUSENKRUG

Map 5; Müller-Breslau-Strasse 14B, Tiergarten;
///estimate.showcase.trumpet; www.schleusenkrug.de

Built on the site of an old lockhouse, this leafy beer garden has been pulling pints since the 1950s, when it served passengers and sailors passing through the canal. Nowadays, Schleusenkrug refreshes those strolling through Tiergarten. There's still a sense of old-school magic to the place, though, with fairy lights draped between trees, chandeliers dangling above the service counter and classics like schnitzel served up. There's no better place to lose track of time.

Breweries and Beer Bars

One of the few things Berlin has in common with the rest of Germany is its intense love of beer. It may be a city of craft beer obsessives, but there will always be a place for traditional Pilsners and wheat varieties.

MÖVE IM FELSENKELLER

Map 5; Akazienstrasse 2, Schöneberg; ///gear.pass.forever; (030) 781 3447

To drink here is to journey back in time. Wood panelling, antique furniture and nautical memorabilia give this smoke-free pub a charm that's unlike the usual nicotine-stained, you're-not-from-round-here *Kneipe* (working man's boozer). Order a well-kept German beer and be regaled by the long-time regulars with tales of a bygone Berlin.

HOPS & BARLEY

**Map 2; Wühlischstrasse 22–3, Friedrichshain;
///messing.fields.rooting; www.hopsandbarley.eu**

Everyone has a soft spot for this Friedrichshain establishment, where pints of the good stuff have been brewed in-house for over a decade. It's the kind of place that works for all manner of crowds:

footie fans getting in a round of Pilsners before a game starts in the back room, couples warming up with a glass of malty *Dunkelbier* (dark beer) in the snug and laidback 9-to-5ers congregating on the street-side tables with a crisp home-brewed cider.

VAGABUND BRAUEREI

Map 6; Antwerpener Strasse 3, Wedding; ///covers.includes.maybe;
www.vagabundbrauerei.com

Founded by three American dudes, Vagabund is the taproom where a smile is guaranteed with your pour — and in Berlin, where service can be hit or miss, that's special. Europe's first crowdfunded brewery is a community stronghold, where strangers-turned-newfound-friends bond over whatever's on tap — maybe a German *helles* (lager), or a Belgian ale. The space itself feels like your uncle's basement bar, with comfy leather barstools and walls so covered in keepsakes (including the crowdfunders' names on the door frame), you can barely see them.

>> **Don't leave without** trying the brewery's own take on a Berlin classic, the cloudy and sour Berliner Weisse.

Try it!
BREW A BEER

The guys behind Vagabund started brewing beer out of an apartment, so who better to learn from? Sign up for a course and learn about beer's main ingredients before getting hands-on yourself.

Solo, Pair, Crowd

In a city this passionate about beer, you're never far from a bar that serves up the good stuff.

FLYING SOLO
Learn the labels

Still getting to know your stout from your pale ale? Head to laidback craft beer haunt Muted Horn in Neukölln, where friendly staff offer up samples to help you find the perfect glass. A shelf of books to choose from will keep you company while you sip.

IN A PAIR
Cosy vibes

Plan a catch-up with a mate at HOME Bar, a UK-inspired pub in Friedrichshain. Order the house pale ale, sink into a sofa and, well, make yourself at home.

FOR A CROWD
Pool and tunes

Friendly competition thrives at Neukölln's funky Bechereck, run by an outgoing Russian landlady. Play your own music through the pool room's laptop and get silly with your group.

PROTOKOLL

**Map 2; Boxhagener Strasse 110, Friedrichshain;
///singing.connects.dusted; www.protokollberlin.de**

Beer geeks are always congregating outside this place, networking
with home brewers and (if they're lucky) craft brewers featured
inside. Protokoll has a penchant for experimental beers from Russia
and the US, but the local brews stocked here are just as good.

» Don't leave without trying a New England IPA from local nomad
brewing heroes Fuerst + Wiacek – Berliners are evangelical about it.

ESCHENBRÄU

Map 6; Triftstrasse 67, Wedding; ///kicks.require.gain; www.eschenbraeu.de

Berlin doesn't do *bierkeller* (beer cellars) *à la* Munich, but down an
unassuming staircase lies the closest thing to basement boozing
you'll get – minus the lederhosen. Run by a self-taught German
brewmaster, this microbrewery prides itself on seasonal homestyle
pints that are unfussy, unfiltered and unbelievably good.

ZEROLIQ

**Map 2; Boxhagener Strasse 104, Friedrichshain;
///educated.enable.topical; www.zeroliq.com**

Sure, Berliners love the taste of a strong dark lager, but today a
sober-curious movement is skyrocketing thanks to health-conscious
locals. There's a lovely relaxed vibe at Germany's first alcohol-free bar,
where friends cosy up and choose between 30 different craft "beers"
– that's more varieties than many alcoholic beer parlours.

Coffee Shops

Berliners can't function without their java (blame lingering withdrawal from the 1970s East German coffee crisis). And with a German woman to thank for inventing the coffee filter, it's basically in their blood.

BONANZA COFFEE ROASTERS

Map 3; Adalbertstrasse 70, Kreuzberg; ///cinemas.womanly.lawful; www.bonanzacoffee.de

There was once a time in Berlin when a caffeine fix mostly came in the form of drip-filtering your own coffee at home. That is until Bonanza entered the coffee shop scene in 2006, pioneering Berlin's third-wave coffee revolution, where sourcing high-quality beans and using top-notch equipment help achieve the best taste.

Try it!
CRAFT A COFFEE

If you want to get more serious about your coffee, take a class at Bonanza. You'll get a great introduction to the science behind the cup, whether it's a workshop on latte art or styles of free-pouring.

You'll find Bonanza's beans in many joints around Berlin, but nothing beats sipping the perfect espresso at their warehouse-like roastery, gazing longingly into the back roasting area.

KAFFEEHAUS KUCHENRAUSCH

Map 2; Simon-Dach-Strasse 1, Friedrichshain; ///froth.choirs.writing; www.kuchenrausch.de

Meeting family and colleagues for *Kaffee und Kuchen*, an afternoon break of coffee and cake, is a long-standing tradition in Germany, but it's one that passes by Berlin's younger generations. This café, however, makes even the coolest of cool kids want to indulge in a slice of it. The perfect combination of hip and traditional, Kaffeehaus KuchenRausch serves up dark, classically strong German coffee with homemade cakes and pies – many gluten-free and vegan.

» Don't leave without trying a classic German *Käsekuchen* (cheesecake), made with curd cheese instead of cream cheese.

WESTBERLIN

Map 4; Friedrichstrasse 215, Kreuzberg; ///proceeds.winners.crisps; www.westberlin-bar-shop.de

It's rare to find a non-chain in Berlin's tourist centre, so artsy coffee shop Westberlin is a real gem. While ranks of selfie sticks dominate Checkpoint Charlie nearby, downtown residents pack into this stylish space to nurse a cappuccino and read a bespoke design magazine – a huge array of which are sold here. Expect a big lunch rush, dogs under tables and a few strollers in the mix.

BEN RAHIM

Map 1; Sophienstrasse 7, Mitte; ///curiosity.terminal.truth; www.benrahim.de

There's not a double-whipped frappé in sight at Ben Rahim, Berlin's first speciality coffee shop with a Middle Eastern twist. Rather, Tunisian-born owner Ben brews his signature Turkish coffee slowly and with precision. Sip it just as leisurely to enjoy the smooth flavours.

CAFÉ IM LITERATURHAUS

Map 5; Fasanenstrasse 23, Charlottenburg; ///trainers.given.coasted;
www.literaturhaus-berlin.de

This 19th-century villa café is a welcome oasis away from nearby shopping avenue Ku'damm. On sunny mornings, senior Berliners retreat to the idyllic garden, pairing a cup of tea with a newspaper. Shoppers join them in the afternoon, resting their pins after hitting all the boulevard's flagships and refuelling with cheesecake and coffee.

» Don't leave without visiting the attached literary salon and bookshop to snag an artsy tome to enjoy with your coffee.

ISLA COFFEE

Map 3; Hermannstrasse 37, Neukölln; ///transit.ditched.couple

In a city of sustainable dining, it was about time someone took the reins of sustainable drinking. Enter zero-waste café Isla Coffee, where the ricotta in the bread pudding you're eating is made from leftover steamed latte milk, and the cup you might be drinking fair-trade coffee in was created from coffee grounds. Settle beside a leafy plant (on a chair made from coffee beans, no less) and welcome some Zen.

Liked by the locals

"We wanted to show that we can always do better, and that the impact we can have doesn't stop when the finished product is on the table. It's part of a cycle in which taste, creativity and value all contribute to a more healthy, sustainable food system."

PETER DURAN, OWNER OF ISLA COFFEE

Dive Bars

Well-worn dive bars are etched into the city's DNA. When it comes to pre-club refreshment or continuing the night into the early hours, it's all about having a good time with cheap drinks and quirky surrounds.

FILMKUNSTBAR FITZCARRALDO

Map 2; Reichenberger Strasse 133, Kreuzberg; ///screamed.chins.amid; www.cinegeek.de/filmkunstbar

The perfect little bad decisions bar, Filmkunstbar is the kind of place where €1 shots of peppermint liqueur (what the locals called "Pfeffi") become an excuse to use up all your spare change. As the hours

Shh!

Friedrichshain's Süss War Gestern *(Wühlischstrasse 43)* is a well-kept secret among youthful circles: students tell their course mates, who bring their dates, who convince their housemates to spend Saturday nights here. There's a living room vibe to the place, where you come to dance to electro or hip hop (depending on the night), sip a cheap beer and play retro video games on a comfy sofa.

get late on the weekend, front-room furniture is cleared away for a makeshift dance floor – the domain of students moving to cheesy pop tunes around rogue piles of jackets.

BEI SCHLAWINCHEN

Map 3; Schönleinstrasse 34, Kreuzberg; ///refers.nickname.bunks; (030) 693 2015

A pandemic was the only thing that could interrupt 40 years of non-stop service at this infamous *Kneipe*. While the bizarre decor is a treat (painted masks, antique toys, a muzzled pig), it's the characterful regulars that make this bar. Order a beer and watch as post-clubbers keep the party alive, old fellas nurse cheap pints at the bar and punks challenge newbies to table football – all in perfect harmony. Exactly the bonkers bunch you'd expect in a 24/7 boozer.

» Don't leave without getting a photo with the (bit creepy) life-size wooden boy sitting in the corner.

MÖBEL OLFE

Map 3; Reichenberger Strasse 177, Kottbusser Tor, Neukölln; ///spaces.swanky.dormant; www.moebel-olfe.de

There's always a party at Berlin's sweatiest LGBTQ+ dive, where locals boogie beneath chairs glued to the ceiling (the space was a former furniture store). Beer comes at a price that won't make you wince come morning – good news considering most of it will end up on the floor amid intense dance sessions. Come Thursday for the legendary (read: crowded) gay nights or Tuesday for the underrated lesbian event.

SCHANKWIRTSCHAFT LAIDAK

Map 3; Boddinstrasse 42–3, Neukölln; ///stutter.digital.elevated;
www.laidak.net

Dive bars don't have to be all grot and beer-soaked oblivion;
they can be intellectual and cosy, too. With shelves of yellowing
classics and tatty sofas, Schankwirtschaft Laidak attracts tortured
academics and frantic freelancers looking to quaff something
inspirational – and cheap cocktails.

MYŚLIWSKA

Map 2; Schlesische Strasse 35, Kreuzberg;
///awakes.odds.smallest; (030) 611 4860

Look, Myśliwska isn't the kind of place you would settle in for the
whole evening – it's smoky, crowded and loud, not to mention the
neon light illuminating the bar. But if you're looking to warm up
before hitting a club, there's nowhere better. Mates rock up to this
intimate, dark spot to start their night, glugging cheap shots with
vim and moving to DJ sets on sticky dance floors.

8MM BAR

Map 1; Schönhauser Allee 177B, Prenzlauer Berg;
///hats.massing.potato; www.8mmmusik.com

This grungy dive bar is a Berlin rock 'n' roll institution. Frequented
by the owner's star-studded friends (think members of Bloc Party
and The Strokes) as well as in-the-know Joes (basically friends, too,
given that the bar staff know most people by name), walking in here

Check 8MM's social pages for a calendar of planned events, from top-notch DJ sets to intimate live performances. feels like stumbling into a backstage after-party. Expect unscripted madness like jam sessions and film screenings, all accompanied by what feels like limitless rounds of cheap beer.

SCHWARZES CAFÉ

Map 5; Kantstrasse 148, Charlottenburg; ///piston.user.orchids;
www.schwarzescafe-berlin.de

When you're after a stripped-back spot to kick back in well-heeled Charlottenburg, look for the lit-up sign of Schwarzes. The peeling paint and exposed weathered brick tell the story of a favourite locale that has been around since the 1970s, when David Bowie and Iggy Pop would pass long nights. It's a safe haven for night owls, where you can order vodka at 10am or coffee at 3am with no judgment from the bartenders or the friendly regulars.

» Don't leave without tucking into the delicious *Apfelstrudel* to soak up that alcohol – and remember to ask for extra cream.

TRINKTEUFEL

Map 3; Naunynstrasse 60, Kreuzberg; ///wiggles.orders.waddled;
www.trinkteufel.de

Tattoos, piercings, a sign declaring "Drink Devil: The Door to Hell" – this legendary dive bar has a rebellious streak. Loud heavy metal plays, pirate decorations line the walls and the crowd of alternative rockers will have you downing soul-inflaming shots in no time.

Wine Bars

There's been something of a wine renaissance of late, with niche gems run by friendly experts popping up across Berlin. When friends plan an overdue catch-up, these classy bars are their hangout of choice.

FREUNDSCHAFT

Map 1; Mittelstrasse 1, Mitte; ///transfers.shocks.wells; www.istdeinbesterfreund.com

Berlin's most respected wine bar attracts the serious, moneyed vino drinkers – but that's not to say it's stuffy. Provocative art, record-player tunes and eccentric Austrian sommeliers keep the vibes at "Friendship" laidback. Nothing beats watching vinophiles in their natural element here, expertly swirling and sniffing their glasses. Blend in by flicking through a leatherbound book of passionately made German and Austrian wines – chin stroking optional.

SHED

Map 3; Pannierstrasse 24, Neukölln; ///wiggly.vouch.pasta; www.1shed.com

Well-kept secrets in trendy Neukölln are hard to come by nowadays, but that's exactly what this unassuming, stylish wine bar is – for now, at least. Serving up deli-style sandwiches by day, Shed dims the lights on the marble tables come evening, when in-the-know twosomes pair natural wines (that's wine made with minimal intervention) with empanadas. The black-beanied sommelier changes the open bottles every night, so there's always something new to try: a sparkling gem from Slovenia or a red from a small-scale vineyard in Central Europe.

BRIEFMARKEN WEINE

**Map 2; Karl-Marx-Allee 99, Friedrichshain; ///intro.bashed.fellow;
www.briefmarkenweine.de**

There's an intensely romantic mood in this tiny Italian spot, housed in a former East German stamp shop. Perhaps it's down to the sexy candlelight, illuminating the couples making eyes at each other over a Tuscan red. Or maybe it's the view of the sun setting over the historic Karl-Marx-Allee while you sip a floral Veneto white. It's old-school charm at its finest, right down to the handwritten menu.

>> **Don't leave without** trying an organic Chardonnay paired with the fresh pasta dish of the day. Bellissimo.

For those who love quantity over quality, Weinerei Forum in Prenzlauer Berg is the ultimate serve-yourself wine bar with a trust-based price concept. Evenings here (it's a café in the day) usher in wine lovers on a budget who "rent" a glass for €2, help themselves to as much wine as they like and pay what they like, too. Berliners are honest people.

Solo, Pair, Crowd

After a glass of vino for one? Or in search of a bottle to share? Berlin has the perfect wine bar for you.

FLYING SOLO
A friendly natter

It's easy to get chatting to owner Andreas at Ottorink, a down-to-earth little bar in Kreuzberg. Ask about the latest young producer he's got on the board, and order by the glass.

IN A PAIR
Get comfy

The most gorgeous of Weserstrasse's "living room bars", Vin Aqua Vin in Neukölln is all about the feel-good vibes. Bring your best pal, settle on a plush sofa and don't leave without buying a bottle for home.

FOR A CROWD
A mini marvel

Gather your mates at Mini in Neukölln for the daily aperitivo: a €5 selection of snacks and glasses of summery Italian rosé. Head here at 5pm to nab a sunny seat in the lounge chairs out front.

ORA

Map 3; Oranienplatz 14, Kreuzberg; ///fondest.hills.burn; www.ora.berlin

Set in a restored 19th-century pharmacy, Ora is easily Berlin's most stunning bar. Yes, the vibe is worldly, but you don't have to be: youthful servers guide you through a list of esoteric natural wines – mostly from lesser-known European regions – with fun stories about volcanic surfaces and funky fermentation. Sommelier Emily is always up to chat about her latest podcast episode, too.

MOTIF WEIN

Map 3; Weserstrasse 189, Neukölln; ///froth.skews.insurers; www.motifwein.de

A natural wine bar for electronic music lovers in Berlin? Naturally. Like-minded souls while away many nights here, huddling around closely seated tables, cradling glasses of sparkling wine, and chatting away between intimate DJ sets and live performances.
» Don't leave without visiting the record shop in the back, where house, funk and disco vinyl is sold until close.

MICHELBERGER

Map 2; Warschauer Strasse 39–40, Friedrichshain; ///mankind.revise.landmark; www.michelbergerhotel.com

This trendy hotel bar has fast become a saviour for after-work revellers finally swapping coffee cups for wine glasses. It's a cosy affair, whether you're sipping cava in the urban courtyard or retreating under a bookshelf with a Riesling.

An evening of cocktails in

eclectic Schöneberg

Beer may reign supreme in Berlin, but a cocktail scene has thrived here since the 1920s. Berlin is, after all, where Christopher Isherwood penned what would later become *Cabaret*, and this spirit of decadence lives on today through, well, spirits (and mixers). Though the city is by no means trapped in the Weimar era, you'll still find pockets of old-school glamour in Schöneberg: Berlin's LGBTQ+ heartland, where sexual freedom and damn good cocktails await. Strap in for a time-travelling bar crawl – just pace yourself.

1. Train Cocktailbar
Hauptstrasse 162,
Schöneberg; www.
traincocktailbar.de
///forever.petition.curry

2. Green Door
Winterfeldtstrasse 50,
Schöneberg; www.green
door.de
///tiny.graceful.gifts

3. Sally Bowles
Eisenacher Strasse 2,
Schöneberg; www.sally-
bowles.de
///tags.monk.stuck

4. Stue Bar
Drakstrasse 1, Schöneberg;
www.so-berlin-das-stue.com
///marriage.walkway.avid

📍 **Nollendorfstrasse 17** ///frocks.assume.league

📍 **Kleine Nachtrevue** ///windy.watch.traffic

HARDENBERGSTRASSE

BREITSCHEID PLATZ

LIETZENBURGER STRASSE

BUNDESALLEE

STRASSE DES 17. JUNI

0 metres 500
0 yards 500

Tiergarten

Enjoy a nightcap at
STUE BAR
End at Das Stue hotel's bar with a
Prohibition-era drink and some live
jazz and swing – if you're lucky.

4

LÜTZOWUFER

Landwehrkanal

DIPLOMATENVIERTEL

Erotic theatre **Kleine
Nachtrevue** *puts on
mash-ups of kinky-
camp performances,
including burlesque
and naked ballet.*

SCHILLSTR.

POTSDAMER STRASSE

WITTENBERG-
PLATZ

KLEISTSTRASSE

*While living in a shared
flat at* **Nollendorfstrasse
17**, *Isherwood met many
characters who inspired
his book,* Goodbye to
Berlin (1939).

Have a bite at
SALLY BOWLES
Tuck into some hearty
German nibbles to a
soundtrack of jazz at this
decadent bar, named after
Cabaret's main character.

3

EISENACHER STR.

2

WINTERFELDTSTRASSE

Seek out
GREEN DOOR
Embrace Prohibition vibes
and ring the bell to enter
this kitschy speakeasy.

HOHENSTAUFENSTRASSE

POTSDAMER STRASSE

YORCKSTRASSE

MARTIN - LUTHER - STRASSE

SCHÖNEBERG

GRUNEWALDSTRASSE

1

Get on board at
TRAIN COCKTAILBAR
Order a caipirinha at this cosy joint,
set in a restored 1920s S-Bahn train.

HAUPTSTRASSE

SHOP

Berlin's shopping scene reflects its conscious locals: marginalized voices shine on bookshelves, vintage trumps fast fashion and local designers are championed.

Record Stores

In a city of DJs, producers and club kids, record stores are holy ground – places to scope out the city's ever-evolving music scene and chart the underground spirit that's prevailed since the 1970s.

HHV

Map 2; Grünberger Strasse 54, Friedrichshain;
///lies.kebab.goes; www.hhv.de

This store started out as a bastion for US hip hop in the 1990s, when importing vinyl from the States was costly and, frankly, took forever to arrive in Germany. Though HHV has since expanded its musical tastes to cover everything from rock to electronic, it still remains hip hop at its core – in part thanks to the cool collection of streetwear and sneakers to rifle through after the digging's done.

BIKINI WAXX

Map 3; Manteuffelstrasse 48, Kreuzberg; ///guessing.pets.gravel;
www.bikiniwaxxrecords.com

Visiting this inconspicuous spot is like popping over to your best mate's flat for an afternoon of tea and tunes. Well, it started out life in an apartment, and the young owners have done a fine job of preserving that living room feel with coffee machines, plush couches, Persian rugs and houseplants. Head upstairs to the cosy loft space to sample your stacks; chances are, there'll be a fellow music fan hanging around to talk Neapolitan disco or Afrofunk with.

» Don't leave without thumbing through the crates for Balearic classics and Italo obscurities.

HARD WAX

Map 3; Paul-Lincke-Ufer 44A, Kreuzberg; ///dish.indoors.door; www.hardwax.com

You don't need to go to Berghain *(p146)* to access Berlin's exclusive dance music scene (plus, Hard Wax is easier to get into). Sitting at the top of a graffitied stairwell, this institution has been pushing Berlin's techno soundscape to a cult-like following since the 1990s. The odd quizzical glance from staff and customers alike can unnerve even the most hardened collectors, but act with purpose and you'll be fine – knowing your Detroit rarities from your dub 45s goes a long way.

Only in Berlin could you find the world's first mobile record store, The Ghost, haunting the streets like a musical mystery machine. The drivers, a Brit DJ duo, sell a great stack of underground house and techno records out the back of a 1970s camper van. You never know where it'll park up next, so keep an eye on the store's social pages for the next appearance.

Liked by the locals

"I've travelled around a bit, but Berlin might be my favourite city to get my hands dirty and dig for vinyl. There are so many hidden gems that, even after eight years, I still seem to stumble upon a magical foxhole every week."

TRISTAN JONG AKA GRATTS,
DJ AND PRODUCER

BIS AUFS MESSER

Map 2; Marchlewskistrasse 107, Friedrichshain; ///spent.thumps.nights; www.bisaufsmesser.com

It's easy to forget that punk and metal have been just as important as synths and drum machines in shaping Berlin's soundscape. This cool little shop flies the flag for that lineage, stocking rare records that span the likes of avant-garde, rock and hardcore genres. If you're naturally averse to the mainstream and into your bands, this is the spot for you.

MELTING POINT

Map 1; Kastanienallee 55, Prenzlauer Berg; ///same.reddish.tonight; (030) 4404 7131

Vinyl junkies who prefer the funkier elements of house music prize this P-Berg store. With records either stacked in piles or stored in cardboard boxes, this no-frills den lets the music do the talking. The owner takes pride in unearthing jewels from local flea markets, so you don't have to.

OYE RECORDS

Map 1; Oderberger Strasse 4, Prenzlauer Berg; ///improve.locating.ranged; www.oye-records.com

Worship at the altar of dance music? Hit up this effortlessly cool spot to snaffle exclusives and hang with acclaimed DJs on Berlin's party circuit – many of whom work here. Loyal fans spend all day here, digging for jazz, afro and hip hop vinyl and awaiting in-store gigs and events.

» Don't leave without chatting to the friendly staff – they're always on hand to answer any question when it comes to tunes, so ask away.

Beloved Markets

The echoes of vendors bartering and inviting displays of organic food define weekends here. Flea and farmers' markets are the lifeblood of Berlin's shopping circuit, bringing out the city's small business spirit.

BOXHAGENER PLATZ

Map 2; Boxhagener Platz, Friedrichshain; ///magnets.standing.cheeses

One person's trash is another's treasure at this Saturday flea market. Cardboard boxes spill over with mismatched china, wonky tables are laden with coffee table curios and old furniture is splayed out haphazardly – yes, shopping here is a disorderly expedition, but you can find great deals. Just ask the students dragging their bargain armchairs home, or the crate digger tightly clutching that rare record. Make your way around the organized chaos and follow your nose to the German sausage stands when it all gets too much.

NOWKOELLN FLOWMARKT

Map 3; Maybachufer 36, Neukölln; ///glue.nibbles.reminder

When Neukölln hipsters want to get rid of their garms, they bring them to this fortnightly Sunday bonanza. And when they want to pick up someone else's knick-knacks, they head right back. There's

Visiting in December? It's a rite of passage to hit up a Christmas market *(p9)* and enjoy a mug of mulled wine.

a real buzz to this canalside market, where live music plays, the scent of street food fills the air and traders hawk local art and obscure collectibles.

SCHILLERMARKT

Map 3; Herrfurthplatz, Neukölln; ///richest.enjoyable.locating

Buying "bio" – aka organic – borders on an obsession in Berlin. But forget hopping from deli to greengrocer to make up that perfect charcuterie board: this Saturday market is full of all the cultivated goods you need. Easy-going locals cradling fresh flowers float between the stands each week, collecting artisanal cheeses for dinner parties and organic breads for Sunday brunches.

TRÖDELMARKT MARHEINEKEPLATZ

Map 4; Bergmannstrasse, Kreuzberg; ///pinks.deeper.grower

This charming jumble market keeps the sophisticated, gentrified Bergmannkiez neighbourhood down to earth. Every weekend, bargain hunters descend to rummage through handmade objects, used books and household goods while the kids eye up the second-hand toys for sale. When the shopping is done, families make their way into the neighbouring indoor Marheineke Markthalle to feast on Spanish tapas (and, for the adults, sip some Italian wine) from top vendors. It's the perfect day out.

» Don't leave without grabbing a glass of rosé from French deli Les Épicuriens and people-watching in the square within the flea market.

STRASSE DES 17. JUNI

Map 5; Strasse des 17. Juni, Tiergarten; ///kickers.poodles.bikers;
www.berlinertroedelmarkt.com

Charlottenburg Gate, Brandenburg Gate's little sister, provides a grand backdrop to this weekend antiques flea market. Watch your elbows, as this is where you'll find the city's most beautiful collectors' relics: timeworn furniture, china, silverware, porcelain. The sellers are serious, seasoned bargainers, so don't interrupt their chess games unless you've really thought through your haggling strategy. Granted, the prices aren't cheap, but the items are of outstanding quality and true Berlin keepsakes set to last another lifetime.

MAUERPARK

Map 1; Mauerpark, Prenzlauer Berg; ///animate.life.vanished

It may be the city's largest Sunday flea market, but one visit to this market and you'll realize the biggest draw is the people-watching. At the entrance, buskers give their all for the materializing crowds, hoping to get discovered. On the park's outer edges, skateboarders

Shh!

Though it's been around for more than eight decades, the Genter Wochenmarkt (*www. wochenmarkt-deutschland.de*) in Wedding still remains under the radar to those living outside the neighbourhood. Boisterous vendors sell cut-price fruit and veg to local customers, sharing banter on first-name terms.

and graffiti artists congregate along the former Berlin Wall, while vendors down below hawk ancient rugs and retro sunnies to thick swarms. Things can get pretty touristy, but local disciples always turn out. After all, where else can you see fire-breathing on a Sunday stroll?

>> Don't leave without singing a song for the famed Bearpit Karaoke at the park's amphitheatre, which becomes a makeshift stage. It's one of the main reasons people head to Mauerpark on a Sunday.

ARENA
Map 2; Eichenstrasse 4A, Alt-Treptow; ///airports.stormy.blend

Praise be for this roofed market, where shopping needn't be cut short because of Berlin's rainy days. Plus, obscure items are packed into every inch of the space, so you'll want to spend a few hours digging and haggling at this weekend flea. Arrive in the morning and bring a few sturdy tote bags – with stalls selling grand chandeliers, ashtrays from the GDR days and so much more, you're guaranteed to leave with things you never knew you wanted, much less need.

MARKT AM WINTERFELDTPLATZ
Map 5; Winterfeldtplatz, Schöneberg; ///plates.attend.wording

This friendly farmers' market is local through and through. The vibe is calm, like the quiet-loving Schönebergers who shop for their groceries on a Saturday. Chat with the traders as you ponder which pungent homemade cheese to buy, splash out on a flower bouquet and stock up on fresh tomatoes. When you've had your fill, settle into a surrounding café and watch the wonderful tableaus of local life.

Sustainable Threads

A Berliner's style may be pretty casual, but locals aren't blasé about where they shop. Looking good while doing good is the aim when digging for vintage staples or watching an artisan upcycle your old garm.

UY STUDIO

Map 3; Pflügerstrasse 11, Neukölln; ///flows.tapers.torn; www.uy-studio.com

This brand's story is classic Berlin: two broke students start making their own clothes, show their threads off at Berghain *(p146)* and, before they know it, their genderless black garms have their very own showroom. A loyal following of revellers sporting leather chokers and heavy eyeliner come here to get kitted out for club nights – think dark edgy fits and fetishy leather gear (vegan, of course). Grab a craft beer from Lager Lager over the road and sip it while you shop (you're allowed).

#DAMUR

Map 3; Reichenberger Strasse 147, Kreuzberg;
///cosmetic.guessing.edit; www.damur.fashion

A brand with a hashtag in it? How millennial – but that's the point. Designer Shih-Shun Huang believes it's up to his generation to question and change today's world, and he's doing this through elegant yet playful clothes at his atelier and showroom. Each unisex collection is a freedom of expression, with bold names like #thisIsTrans and #YouAreNotBlackEnough aiming to challenge the status quo. Add to that an upcycling approach (he created a collection entirely from previous seasons' stock fabric), and #DAMUR could well change the world – or over-production in the fashion industry, at least.

CAPT'N CROP

Map 3; Reuterstrasse 52, Neukölln; ///shares.withdrew.snippet;
www.captn-crop.com

At this dual workroom and shop, modern-day mad hatters make cool hats from found and recycled materials. This is where your new favourite cap was sewn from your neighbours' old Levi's and that bucket hat you never take off was crafted from your grandfather's old curtains. Every piece is unique, cut and sewn by cap-wearing artisans between their deserved beer breaks outside.

» **Don't leave without** choosing a fabric and asking the designers to make you something from scratch. They make bags and belts, too.

Try it!
LEARN TO SEW

Inspired by Berlin's artisans? Take an easy alteration and repair workshop in English with Wieder & Wider (www.wiederundwider. com) and learn to either fix or upcycle old garments on a sewing machine.

Liked by the locals

"The Berlin style is all about being yourself and feeling free in whatever you want to do. We're trying to create the perfect garments to elevate this experience and get you ready for the best clubbing experience."

IWAN BIJKERK,
MARKETING MANAGER AT NAKT

NAKT STUDIO

Map 3; Sonnenallee 120, Neukölln; ///fails.flock.pylons; www.nakt-studio.com

Look cool, dress in black and show some skin – locals know the unwritten rules of club fashion by heart, and NAKT helps them achieve them. This techno fashion label empowers a community of ravers (aka the NAKT ARMY) through sharp cuts, minimalist designs and metallic accessories, which make getting into KitKat Club *(p147)* a breeze.

MADE IN BERLIN

Map 1; Neue Schönhauser Strasse 19, Mitte; ///chain.shout.reapply; www.picknweight.de

A Berliner's style doesn't start and end at black garms: they're also partial to a tracksuit and funky jumper, and the city's original vintage shop is the place to mop up such 1980s and 90s fashions. A browse is always a pleasure, but serious bargain hunters time their visit on a Tuesday, when it's 20 per cent off between 12 and 3pm.

SHIO

Map 3; Weichselstrasse 59, Neukölln; ///speeches.soft.prove; www.shiostore.com

Find that second-hand garms never fit you right? This little store was created with you in mind. Owner Kate produces everything in the studio's backroom, retailoring flea market items and producing new garments from recycled fabrics, like former GDR cotton bedsheets.

» Don't leave without checking out the other designers who share the shop with Kate, producing jewellery and decorative books.

Home Touches

Much like self-styling, apartment dressing in Berlin leans towards cobbled together and shabby-chic. As long as it's characterful, made with TLC and won't be found in your mate's house too, Berliners are all for it.

FOLKDAYS

Map 2; Manteuffelstrasse 19, Kreuzberg;
///diplomat.maximum.muddle; www.folkdays.com

In a city of multicultural artists, a store like Folkdays makes sense – a single place to shop for artisan pieces from global craftspeople, all of whom decide their own prices. A dedicated following of hipster mamas go gaga for the minimalist, handmade and fair-trade items, like recycled glassware from a Cairo-based glassblower and delicate ceramics made in India and Thailand.

BIKINI BERLIN

Map 5; Budapester Strasse 38–50, City West;
///towns.mascots.curl; www.bikiniberlin.de

You never know what you're going to get at Germany's first concept mall, except that it'll always be one of a kind. Here, pop-up boxes are rented by independent fashion and homeware designers that

 If you're liking Berlin's epic department stores, hit up famed KaDaWe nearby to do some luxury shopping. tend to come and go from one month to the next. Expect a store selling too-cool-to-burn twist candles on one visit and rocket-shaped decanters the next.

MANUFACTUM

Map 5; Hardenbergstrasse 4–5, Charlottenburg;
///tangible.cleans.long; www.manufactum.de

Local sustainable brands were hard to come by in Berlin until a Green Party member opened this store three decades ago, selling household goods made from environmentally friendly materials. It still has the low-down on the best Made in Germany brands: natural soaps, luxurious Lamy fountain pens and wood-carved everything. Whether you buy a yak wool throw or steel knives forged at Königsmünster Abbey, it'll be timeless and durable (okay, granted, the soaps won't last forever).

STILWERK

Map 5; Kantstrasse 17, Charlottenburg; ///crawled.shirts.shifting;
www.stilwerk.com

Housing 55 shops, this sleek department store is where design junkies come to kit out their home offices with slinky lamps and barely-there ergonomic chairs. While the prices tend to be, well, pricey, soaking up inspiration on how to reconfigure your living room or hearing about the latest trends at a Saturday talk is all delightfully free.

» Don't leave without heading up to the roof terrace on the fifth floor for a fantastic view over Berlin and even more inspiration.

HALLESCHES HAUS
Map 4; Tempelhofer Ufer 1, Kreuzberg; ///terminal.faced.parks;
www.hallescheshaus.com

Though the American-Brit owners quit the corporate world to open Hallesches Haus, they still brought a touch of office life with them. Blending coworking with shopping, this general store/café is a hub for creatives who peruse the shelves between bursts of typing and cake nibbling. No laptop? No problem; simply pop by to pick up perfect suitcase stuffers like macramé plant hangers, hand-poured candles, cutesy ring holders and even funky vibrators.

VIELFACH
Map 4; Zimmerstrasse 11, Das Kreativkaufhaus, Mitte;
///pens.mondays.land; www.geschenke-berlin.com

Buying local acquires a whole new meaning at this unique showroom. Over 100 German designers and artists rent display space for their homemade merch here, providing Berliners with the holy grail: a place to buy a gift for their sister, father and great aunt all at the same time.

Try it!
GET SKETCHING

If all these design stores ignite the inner artist in you, book onto a class with Drink and Draw Berlin *(www.drinkanddrawberlin. com)*. You'll produce your own art piece to take home while enjoying a tipple.

Realistically, you'll come to buy an art print for a friend's birthday and leave with ceramics for yourself to show off at a dinner party (and a new bag, because you need something to take them home in, right?).

VEB ORANGE

Map 1; Oderberger Strasse 29, Prenzlauer Berg;
///exposing.vivid.seasons; www.veborange.de

Sure, a minimalist aesthetic of clean lines and muted tones has taken Berlin's apartments by storm, but there was a time when homes in this uber cool epicentre actually dipped their toe in a colour palette. The proof? VEB Orange, a vintage shop dedicated to kitsch decor from 1960s and 70s East Germany. Retro curios hark back to a vibrant and camp design era: geometric-patterned lamps, multi-hued rotary phones, and – no surprises here – a whole lot of orange. It truly satisfies the feeling of *Ostalgie* (nostalgia for East Germany).

DIE ESPRESSIONISTEN

Map 4; Zimmerstrasse 90, Mitte; ///grazed.inhales.behind;
www.espressionisten.de

If there's one staple item on a Berliner's kitchen counter, it's a coffee press – and this shop-meets-café takes that addiction to the next level. Between milk steaming and tending to customers' machine repairs, the staff help old- and new-timers pick out espresso-making gear, presses, and stylish cups and tamps from the floor-to-ceiling shelves.

» Don't leave without ordering a coffee, of course – then buying the beans to make a cup at home with your new equipment.

Book Nooks

Forget the mainstream: Berliners bypass characterless corporates for charming independents, where niche coffee table books, thought-provoking fiction and political tomes feed their topical interests.

ANOTHER COUNTRY

Map 4; Riemannstrasse 7, Kreuzberg; ///inched.vipers.altitude; www.anothercountry.de

Quirky Brit Sophia was onto a good thing when she opened this spot, now Berlin's most beloved English-language bookshop. This expat enclave is a home away from home: a cosy chaos of used books stacked across shelves hints at a home library, reading circles inspire

Shh!

Another Country's little sister, The.Word (*Willmanndamm 4*) is a much-needed newbie on the scene. A literature café and lending library, it has a special focus on books about BIPOC, LGBTQ+ and minority experiences, and prides itself on being an inclusive space. In-the-know fans stalk socials for the events, like spoken word nights or swing dance classes.

new and long-time Berliners to mingle with beers, and dinner parties see Sophia serve up home-cooked dishes. Topping it all off is a "buy or borrow system", where you can take a book for keeps, or pay the price and get a refund (minus a €1.50 borrowing fee) upon return.

SAINT GEORGE'S

Map 1; Wörther Strasse 27, Prenzlauer Berg;
///juror.light.cultivation; www.saintgeorgesbookshop.com

Spend enough time trawling the shelves here and you'll chance upon a well-thumbed classic that takes you back to your student days, or the rare poetry collection that you've spent weeks searching for. Somehow, it feels like the stock was curated just for you, so sink into the big chesterfield at the back and let the hours pass by with your purchase.

PRO QM

Map 1; Almstadtstrasse 48, Mitte;
///displays.hushed.acrobat; www.pro-qm.de

Picture this: it's the 1990s, a trio of artists spend hours having debates on urban politics, and an idea strikes. That idea was Pro qm, a thematic bookstore with a focus on the city, where people can freely engage in topics of urban development, architecture and the economy. Flash forward to the 2020s and this minimalist space is the domain of stylish Mitte types seeking an intellectual fix. The catalogue, which focuses on politics, design and photography, is Berlin defined.

>> Don't leave without asking about the events calendar – the store tends to hold regular book presentations and even exhibitions.

EISENHERZ

Map 5; Motzstrasse 23, Schöneberg; ///marbles.happier.twisty;
www.prinz-eisenherz.buchkatalog.de

Founded by gay activists in 1978, this collective-owned store was
Germany's first openly gay bookshop. It continues to stand proud
as a hub for Berlin's LGBTQ+ community, stocking gay and lesbian
books and comics, and exhibiting the work of queer artists.

» Don't leave without chatting to the friendly co-owners Franz and
Roland. They know a lot about the area's gay history, and the many
magazines and films that have been planned within the shop's walls.

MOTTO BERLIN

Map 2; Skalitzer Strasse 68, Kreuzberg;
///fraction.stepping.explores; www.mottodistribution.com

It's fitting that a store with such a prized catalogue of photography,
art and design publications is housed in an old frame workshop.
Clued-up arty types and designers spend hours flicking through
the rare editions and fashion zines they've just purchased, lingering
for an evening talk or screening to get underway.

SHAKESPEARE AND SONS

Map 2; Warschauer Strasse 74, Friedrichshain;
///flooding.kind.kingdom; www.shakespeareandsons.com

Books, bagels and caffeine – Shakespeare and Sons has your morning
sorted. The English-language bookstore is an oasis for literature-
loving expats, all captivated by the smells of new print editions and

Owner Lauren of Fine Bagels holds the odd challah and bagel-making class. Check socials for details.

fresh baking from the café, Fine Bagels. With a cappuccino, chocolate babka and the latest page-turner, time blissfully stands still.

SHE SAID

Map 3; Kottbusser Damm 79, Neukölln; ///engaging.tides.sculpture; www.shesaid.de

This bookstore was an instant hit when it opened in 2020 – you only need to look at the queue of bibliophiles out front to confirm it. Sure, many bookstores in liberal Berlin stock a number of female and queer authors, but this minimalist shop goes one step further: dedicating a whole space to lesser-represented voices in the fiction, non-fiction and children's categories. The passionate staff are always up for a natter about undiscovered gems – chances are, you'll leave armed with a new book to shout about.

DUSSMANN DAS KULTURKAUFHAUS

Map 1; Friedrichstrasse 90, Mitte; ///cheeses.slamming.stealing; www.kulturkaufhaus.de

Dussmann is far more than just a place to shop. This huge space is a sanctuary for like-minded readers who discuss the latest novel over coffee in the vertical garden, get recommendations from passionate staff and tune in to cultural discussions at regular events. You'll nip in quickly only to find hours have flown by and you can't even remember what you came in for, but that's half the joy.

Mooch around
ORIGINAL IN BERLIN

Mid-20th-century furniture your thing? Browse the collection of chairs, tables and more at this museum-like store and you'll soon be rethinking your whole flat.

Get kitted out at
HUMANA SECONDHAND & VINTAGE

Take your time rooting for your next clubbing outfit at Europe's largest second-hand store.

FRIEDENSTRASSE

PETERSBURGER STR

WEIDENWEG

RIGAER

KARL-MARX-ALLEE

KOPPENSTRASSE

STRASSE DER PARISER KOMMUNE

FRIEDRICHSHAIN

RÜDERSDORFER STRASSE

WARSCHAUER STRASSE

The socialist boulevard **Karl-Marx-Allee** was a shopping paradise in the GDR, with shops selling items that were not available elsewhere.

2

3

KOPERNIKUSSTR.

SIMON-DACH-STRASSE

1

Peruse the stalls at
ANTIKMARKT AM OSTBAHNHOF

If it's a Sunday, revel in the feeling of *Ostalgie* (nostalgia for East Germany) at this huge flea, where stalls brim with the likes of old coins and advertising posters.

Expressing yourself through clothing plays a big part in whether you get into notorious club **Berghain** (p146). *So does wearing black.*

4

Get inspired at
STUDIO K.W.D

Watch the ateliers at work while you browse this studio/shop, where used materials like bicycle wheels are upcycled into cool accessories.

MÜHLENSTRASSE

Spree

MERCEDES-PLATZ

0 metres	400
0 yards	400

A morning of
vintage shopping

Berliners are serious thrifters – weekends are spent haggling at flea markets, flats are decked out in second-hand furniture and club outfits are the result of hours spent trawling vintage stores. Many deem Neukölln the city's vintage hub, but Friedrichshain is hot on its heels, home to two big flea markets and many lesser-known gems. There's no better way to start a morning than ambling through this former socialist heartland.

1. Antikmarkt am Ostbahnhof
Erich-Steinfurth-Strasse 1, Friedrichshain; (030) 2900 2010
///animate.bridges.averts

2. Original in Berlin
Karl-Marx-Allee 83, Friedrichshain; www.originalinberlin.com
///avid.thus.shoebox

3. HUMANA Secondhand & Vintage
Frankfurter Tor 3, Friedrichshain; www.humana-second-hand.de
///speaking.rocker.slams

4. Studio K.W.D
Libauer Strasse 1, Friedrichshain; www.kwd.berlin
///dollar.shiver.caller

5. Vinyl-a-GoGo
Krossener Strasse 24, Friedrichshain; www.vinyl-a-gogo.de
///wept.croak.headset

📍 **Karl-Marx-Allee**
///trader.salutes.lake

📍 **Berghain**
///period.talkers.crystals

Rifle through VINYL-A-GOGO
Hip hop, jazz, African funk: it's all here. Find a new favourite jam at this second-hand gem.

ARTS & CULTURE

A haven for creatives, Berlin is shaped by artistic expression. While the past can never be forgotten, locals write new stories with vibrant street art and radical theatre.

City History

Berlin wouldn't be the place of solidarity it is today without its eclectic past. Between the bullet holes in the buildings (yes, really) are sites that celebrate a city of survivors and its triumphs.

BAUHAUS-ARCHIV

Map 5; Klingelhöferstrasse 14, Schöneberg;
///briskly.invent.goggles; www.bauhaus.de

Though only around for a flash, Bauhaus was the zeitgeist-defining art school that truly shaped the Weimar Republic. A century on and its modernist work still resonates with design devotees, who flock to this archive to fawn over its legacy. Drawings, manuscripts, furniture and everything in between are housed in a sawtooth-roofed museum designed by Walter Gropius, the movement's idolized founder.

REFUGEE VOICE TOURS

Map 4; Wilhelmstrasse 45, Mitte; ///shelters.dishing.lipstick;
www.refugeevoicetours.org

Back in 2015, the words "migrant crisis" hogged every headline, but it wasn't until Refugee Voice Tours that Berlin's newcomers could control their narrative. On a walking tour of Berlin's landmarks, charismatic

End the tour with your group at Mandi Restaurant, sharing more stories over Syrian dishes for €8. guides draw parallels between Syria and Germany – both countries where civil unrest has forced citizens to flee. It's mighty eye-opening, and a chance to reflect.

SCHWULES MUSEUM

Map 5; Lützowstrasse 73, Schöneberg; ///urgent.member.inclined; www.schwulesmuseum.de

In a city where being yourself is celebrated, the Gay Museum, the world's first dedicated to LGBTQ+ history, just makes sense. Four ever-changing exhibition spaces chart key moments within Berlin's LGBTQ+ culture and beyond, like the life of former East Germany's gay icon Charlotte von Mahlsdorf and the queer history of video games. Exhibits aside, the evening talks cover everything from coming out stories to philosophy, keeping open-minded crowds coming back.

STASI MUSEUM

Map 6; Normannenstrasse 20/Haus 1, Lichtenberg; ///country.slave.husbands; www.stasimuseum.de

The GDR's former state security HQ is a symbol of both oppression and liberty for East Berliners. Its story is as local as it gets: in January 1990 angry activists stormed the building, prising it from the crumbling regime as officials frantically destroyed documents inside. Many files were saved, and provide a chilling insight into the Stasi's spy tactics here.

» Don't leave without visiting the eerie stillness of Stasi head honcho Erich Mielke's old office, restored to its original condition.

BERLIN WALL MEMORIAL
Map 1; Bernauer Strasse 111, Mitte; ///uniform.farms.odds;
www.berliner-mauer-gedenkstaette.de

You can't value the freedom in Berlin today without recalling the wall that divided the East and West for 28 years, and this remaining stretch remembers the lives claimed of those fleeing East Germany. Two figures embracing outside the Chapel of Reconciliation reflect how Berliners feel when visiting – solemn, but finally reunited.

CLÄRCHENS BALLHAUS
Map 1; Auguststrasse 24, Mitte; ///protects.november.barn;
www.claerchensball.haus

One of Berlin's remaining relics of the 1920s, this ballroom has survived two world wars and a divided city – hey, if the walls could talk, they'd have plenty to say. Movers and shakers still come to tango the night away in the *Spiegelsaal*, a grand mirrored dance hall of crumbling stuccos and peeling paint. Its faded elegance is at its best under the glow of candlelight; seeing it empty during the day feels like being a hundred years late for the last dance.

BUCHSTABENMUSEUM
Map 5; Stadtbahnbogen 424, Hansaviertel;
///retail.camp.computer; www.buchstabenmuseum.de

Berliners will tell you this is a city that's always evolving, and nowhere exemplifies its ever-changing nature quite like the quirky Letter Museum. Home to over a thousand salvaged letters, logos and placards that (mostly) adorned the city's old buildings, this is an A–Z of a Berlin lost to change and gentrification. It's where long-time locals rediscover the signage from the stores they visited as a kid, and typography nerds read the origin story of the city's oldest neon sign.

» **Don't leave without** seeing the giant "E" that made it onto the set of Quentin Tarantino's *Inglorious Basterds*.

GEDENKSTÄTTE BERLIN-HOHENSCHÖNHAUSEN

Map 6; Genslerstrasse 66, Alt-Hohenschönhausen;
///exulted.conga.extra; www.stiftung-hsh.de

A former Soviet and Stasi prison isn't for everyone, but cast aside your doubts and book a tour of this memorial. Removed from official maps for 44 years, it still feels like a no-man's land, located on an austere business estate. Guides, many of whom are former prisoners, walk you through the complex while describing the tortuous techniques their jailers used, shining a light on political persecution in East Germany.

Shh!

With its malls and corporate skyscrapers, Potsdamer Platz can be a bit dry – unless you know where to look. The old GDR watchtower on Erna-Berger-Strasse is the last of its kind, while the pentagonal signal tower is a replica of Europe's first traffic light, erected here in 1924, long before Berlin's beloved Ampelmann crossed the road.

Alternative Galleries

What do you do with a disused brewery or squat? Turn it into an art gallery, of course. Berlin is a city for and by artists, where social infrastructure supports creativity and galvanizes a boundary-pushing scene.

SAMMLUNG BOROS

Map 1; Reinhardtstrasse 20, Mitte; ///universe.highs.clocks;
www.sammlung-boros.de

Given how much Berlin worships the underground, a contemporary art gallery in a World War II bunker just fits. True to that underground spirit, this isn't the easiest place to get into: you can only visit as part of a pre-booked tour, and only 12 guests are allowed at one time. Made it inside? Enjoy rotating works by international artists like Damian Hirst and Olafur Eliasson.

KUNTSRAUM BETHANIEN

Map 3; Mariannenplatz 2, Kreuzberg; ///arrived.names.fountain;
www.kunstraumkreuzberg.de

When this hospital shut in 1970, a battle erupted to save the building from demolition. Squatters and conservationists won out, and what's now a contemporary art space has been challenging the powers that be ever since. Expect headline-worthy exhibitions that highlight social-political dilemmas like climate change or the international arms trade. One for those who believe art is protest.

» Don't leave without taking an open studio tour for a peek inside the artist ateliers and striking up a chat about the state of the world.

KW INSTITUTE FOR CONTEMPORARY ART

Map 1; Auguststrasse 69, Scheunenviertel, Mitte;
///reshape.rapport.breathed; www.kw-berlin.de

In the 1990s, a former margarine factory became a contemporary art space with one rule: no permanent exhibitions. Since then, KW has been the vanguard of the Berlin creative scene, responding to shifting trends in the art world. The non-profit is all about exhibiting fresh artists and out-there installations – you know, an exploration of sex dolls and robots, or an artist's hypnotherapy session – while still honouring older contemporaries. Reflect on it all at the adjoining café.

FREIRAUM IN DER BOX

Map 2; Boxhagener Strasse 93, Friedrichshain;
///feeds.speeches.sprays; www.freiraum-berlin.org

Only free-spirited Berliners could have imagined a radical art space like this one. Housed inside a former stables, Freiraum takes a swing at exploring identity, diversity and sustainability through installations, photography and sculptures. Eco-warriors and political activists unite here, pondering the works and attending urban talks.

KÖNIG GALERIE

Map 4; Alexandrinenstrasse 118–21, Kreuzberg;
///overlook.rabble.sobbed; www.koeniggalerie.com

Don't be fooled by the name of art dealer Johan König's self-titled gallery: this isn't his vanity project. Rather, exhibitions at this brutalist church are about promoting the next generation of artists – easy, given that the monotone grey interior is the perfect blank canvas for sculpture, video and paint works. It's a magnet for curious art students.

HOŠEK CONTEMPORARY

Map 1; Fischerinsel 3, MS Heimatland, Mitte; ///acute.tulip.offices;
www.hosekcontemporary.com

Combine Berlin's love of galleries and water and you get Hošek, an art residency on the restored cargo ship MS *Heimatland*. From March to October, it's a hotspot for free-wheeling creatives discussing the experimental sound installations and relaxing on the Spree.

HAMBURGER BAHNHOF

Map 5; Invalidenstrasse 50–51, Mitte; ///exposing.capacity.pass;
www.smb.museum

This railway station-turned-gallery has become synonymous with Berlin's modern art scene. It's the only place any self-respecting Pop Art or Expressionism fan comes for an ever-changing fill of Andy Warhol, Cy Twombly and Sigmar Polke.

>> Don't leave without visiting the restaurant for homemade fare: coffee and cake baked in-house, or fish smoked on-site.

Liked by the locals

"Curating a programme in such a unique space is exciting and challenging – you have to be fearless. We've achieved complete freedom in our artistic choices, while also creating a strong community through our work with international artists."

LINDA TOIVIO, CURATOR AT HOŠEK CONTEMPORARY

Favourite Museums

When a city has a whole island dedicated to museums,
you know it means business. But it doesn't stop there.
Across Berlin, world-class institutions and esoteric
collections honour the past and celebrate the present.

GROPIUS BAU

Map 4; Niederkirchnerstrasse 7, Kreuzberg; ///homing.lance.tallest;
www.berlinerfestspiele.de/en/gropiusbau

This is a heavyweight in Berlin's art world. Poised on the old fault line
between East and West, the palace-like Gropius Building has a history
worthy of its own exhibition. Speaking of exhibits, the shows here are
always the talk of the town – being able to say you saw Yayoi Kusama's
polka dots (and bagging the picture to prove it) is as crucial as
appreciating the contemporary art on display.

NEUES MUSEUM

Map 1; Bodestrasse 1–3, Museumsinsel, Mitte;
///rosier.scramble.snapped; www.smb.museum

It may be called the New Museum, but Berliners love irony. They also
love classical antiquities. Sure, this stalwart's stucco-coated limestone
bust of Nefertiti is cool and all, but there's so much more here. While

 Get the Welcome Card for Museum Island for access to the five museums and public transport.

gaggling kids crowd around the queen, steer your history-loving pals towards the wall paintings of Nordic mythological scenes and artifacts from Troy.

COMPUTERSPIELEMUSEUM

Map 2; Karl-Marx-Allee 93A, Friedrichshain; ///wording.vipers.needed; www.computerspielemuseum.de

Brimming with retro consoles and video games, the colourful nerd utopia that is the Computer Games Museum takes you on a serious nostalgia trip, its themed rooms charting the evolution of gaming culture over the last six decades. While your dad raves about a Nimrod model and your niece discovers SuperMario, pop on a pair of 3D glasses and let a virtual reality game take you into the future.

PERGAMON MUSEUM

Map 1; Bodestrasse 1–3, Museumsinsel, Mitte; ///modes.animal.flagged; www.smb.museum

This is Museum Island's big one – you know, the one that your mum is desperate to visit when she's in town. Unbearably long queues and endless selfie snappers are enough to let your mum down gently, but don't: the Islamic carpets, Iranian jewellery and Roman architecture really are worth the hype. Just book a ticket online for a weekday morning and ponder the antiquities before the stomping groups arrive.

» Don't leave without seeing the beautiful blue Ishtar Gate of Babylon, which the Iraqi government is keen to get repatriated.

MUSEUM DER DINGE

**Map 3; Oranienstrasse 25, Kreuzberg; ///puzzled.opera.arena;
www.museumderdinge.de**

Think the ennui of daily life is a drag? Visit the Museum of Things. Hidden in an old factory is this archive of everyday items designed by the Deutscher Werkbund, a collective committed to revolutionizing cultural life through design. Shelves of fondue sets, tobacco tins and snow globes give an insight into how objects have both shaped and been shaped by our changing consumer needs (oh, capitalism). It's the most fun you can have in a room of electric kettles and GDR toiletries.

MUSEUM FÜR NATURKUNDE

**Map 1; Invalidenstrasse 43, Mitte; ///punchy.steers.steep;
www.museumfuernaturkunde.berlin**

The Museum of Natural History is worth visiting for many reasons, and a 12-m- (39-ft-) high Giraffatitan skeleton is the biggest – literally. It's impressive during the day, but a whole other world

Unbeknown to those who wander through the Museum of Natural History, it's not all magnified insect models and uber-rare proto-bird bones. Behind the scenes, budding and expert creatives take part in nude drawing sessions and watercolour classes that aim to bring the collection to life. Check the website for dates and further information.

opens up on weekend evenings, when the museum gates close and Torchlight Tours commence. It's pretty special spying taxidermied polar bears under the cover of darkness.

MUSEUM FÜR FOTOGRAFIE

Map 5; Jebensstrasse 2, City West; ///good.stuff.romance;
www.smb.museum

Hidden inside a former Prussian officers' casino, the Museum of Photography is sacred ground for camera-wielding locals. Serious snappers worship the erotic black-and-whites from late fashion photographer Helmut Newton, students ponder war shots taken by James Nachtwey and accompanying lectures build a community of passionate photographers and photojournalists.

» **Don't leave without** visiting the "Helmut Newton's Private Property" exhibit, filled with images and cameras donated by Berlin-born Newton.

JÜDISCHES MUSEUM

Map 4; Lindenstrasse 9–14, Kreuzberg;
///refrain.admits.because; www.jmberlin.de

For Berlin's growing Jewish community, the the Jewish Museum is a place to comprehend and contemplate their identity. A thousand years of Jewish history culminates in this quiet space, where a toy carried in a girl's suitcase when fleeing to England recalls the tragedies of World War II; listening pods bring intimate biographical tales to life; and powerful photographs show Germany today through the eyes of Jewish contemporary artists.

Performing Arts

Theatre, dance, spoken word, string instruments:
there's no limit to how Berliners express themselves.
Whether it's about pushing boundaries or honouring
the classical arts, the creative scene is multifaceted.

STAATSOPER UNTER DEN LINDEN

Map 1; Unter den Linden 7, Mitte; ///guitars.chills.filer;
www.staatsoper-berlin.de

For all their techno and punk music proclivities, Berliners are partial to a bit of Beethoven – and truly proud of their famous State Opera House. When the grandiose 18th-century building warmly lights up at night, denizens of high culture filter in to baroque rafters, awaiting stellar singers and fabulous acoustics. Some dress up, some don't, but you've likely splurged on a ticket, so why not don your best?

TEMPODROM

Map 4; Möckernstrasse 10, Kreuzberg; ///hung.synthetic.guitar;
www.tempodrom.de

Circus by appearance, circus by nature, this soaring tent-like venue is where idiosyncratic talents come to entertain. There's always something going on: a stand-up comic making their Berlin debut, a

Return to Tempodrom to visit Liquidrom, a cool on-site spa with coloured lights and underwater speakers. | classic Russian ballet welcoming in the festive period or an actual circus dazzling the masses. It's one for the planners, so book ahead for an unforgettable night.

SCHAUBÜHNE

Map 5; Kurfürstendamm 153, City West; ///bonus.thanks.dominate; www.schaubuehne.de

The Schaubühne (literally, Theatre) has a reputation that exceeds Germany itself, let alone Berlin's circles of theatre lovers. Yes, Thomas Ostermeier is a well-regarded artistic director, and, yes, the ensemble includes film stars, but there's nothing showy about the classic venue, nor the experimental and contemporary plays shown here. The focus is purely on the captivating acting, passionate storytelling and the hard-hitting emotions you're guaranteed to feel.

» Don't leave without enquiring about the shows and times when English or French surtitles are available.

F40

Map 4; Fidicinstrasse 40, Kreuzberg; ///tenders.actor.latter; www.thikwa.de, www.etberlin.de

This tiny theatre space doubles up on its repertoire. It's a home for English Theatre Berlin, the city's only company to exclusively perform original and well-known plays in English. And it's also home to Thikwa, a collaborative theatre by disabled and non-disabled actors who put on experimental journeys across music, spoken word and dance.

BERLINER PHILHARMONIKER

Map 4; Herbert-von-Karajan-Strasse 1, Tiergarten;
///examine.tennis.respects; www.berliner-philharmoniker.de

Despite its global renown, the Berlin Philharmonic is dedicated to making orchestral music accessible to all walks of life. Tickets to shows are affordable (€15, a bargain), but for cent-watching students and hungry musicians, the free lunchtime concerts are a saviour. Settle into the foyer every Wednesday between September and June to watch acclaimed musical luminaries do their thing.

BALLHAUS NAUNYNSTRASSE

Map 3; Naunynstrasse 27, Kreuzberg; ///cars.compound.gearbox;
www.ballhausnaunynstrasse.de

A performing arts centre with a sole focus on BIPOC and queer perspectives isn't easy to find in Germany, which is why this one is so important. Thought-provoking shows, created by young talents, focus on personal experiences: past works include solo dance piece *New Growth*, about one woman's interrogation of the politics around Black hair, and *Complex of Tensions*, a play about the experiences of queer Black men living in Berlin. English surtitles are available if you ask.

MAXIM GORKI

Map 1; Am Festungsgraben 2, Mitte; ///capers.scrum.asteroid; www.gorki.de

Known for producing experimental "post-migrant theatre", Maxim Gorki makes it its mission to celebrate Berlin's multicultural side and promote inclusivity. Surtitled in English, the original productions here always explore varying facets of identity (think queer love stories, performative journeys of the Roma experience or modern retellings of Dostoyevsky's works). The space may be small, but its performances have a lot to say – and you will too, so join the fellow thespians debating in the canteen after watching a show. It's a theatre that's as inviting and warm as it is eye-opening and socially engaging.

HAU

Map 4; Hallesches Ufer 32, Kreuzberg; ///club.trips.proofs;
www.hebbel-am-ufer.de

In true avant-garde style, you can expect to see HAU's provocative posters plastered on graffitied walls and light poles all over Berlin. And the shows at this edgy English-language theatre are just as in your face. Here, the lines between theatre, dance, music and art are blurred to ask the all-important questions, like "what does a post-apocalyptic world look like?" and "why are we so reliant on fossil fuels?".
» Don't leave without heading to the theatre's WAU pub, where the makers of the show you just watched will probably be hanging out.

Try it!
DO A DANCE

Two left feet? Tanzfabrik *(www.tanzfabrik-berlin.de)* will right that. This contemporary dance school offers lessons in English, so book into a beginner's class and learn to express yourself.

Street Art

Rest assured that if there's a postwar derelict building left unembellished, there's a tagger spraying it. Street art goes deep in Berlin, symbolizing that hard-earned freedom of expression that locals cherish.

TEUFELSBERG

Map 6; Teufelsseechaussee 10, Grunewald; ///roofs.flaked.exists; www.teufelsberg-berlin.de

Berlin has a habit of blowing your mind at every turn, and Teufelsberg is no exception. Built on a mountain of postwar rubble, this former Cold War spy station was where the NSA would eavesdrop behind the Iron Curtain. Since decommissioning, it's gone from keeping tabs to showcasing tags, its ruins and radar domes plastered with

Try it!
GRAB A CAN

Book a graffiti workshop at Mauerpark, a well-known spot for street artists near a former stretch of the Berlin Wall. You'll spend the afternoon learning spray-painting techniques from a pro.

poignant murals. Meandering through may feel like trespassing (amped up by an eerie sound installation), but rest assured the only eyes watching are from a surreal, vibrant portrait.

HAUS SCHWARZENBERG COMPLEX

**Map 1; Rosenthaler Strasse 39, Mitte; ///plunger.tank.fence;
www.haus-schwarzenberg.org**

This grungy alleyway is an island in Mitte's sea of gentrification. The unassuming entrance is easily missed unless you know what's within: crumbling walls emblazoned with posters, stickers and colourful graffiti, worshipped by boho denizens passing through. Local artists bomb the walls on a weekly basis, but the shimmering portrait of Anne Frank by UK-based Jimmy C remains respectfully untouched.

EAST SIDE GALLERY

**Map 2; Mühlenstrasse 3–100, Friedrichshain;
///scope.partied.possibly; www.eastsidegalleryberlin.de**

No place represents Berlin quite so much as the East Side Gallery. It's in the city's blood to reinvent tragedy with creativity and hope, and that's what this former stretch of the Berlin Wall — the world's largest open-air gallery — has done since 1990. Here, a collection of graffiti and social commentary perfectly captures the rebellious nature of modern street art and Berlin itself. Yes, it's touristy, but locals still can't resist biking by and seeing what's new among the selfie snappers.

» Don't leave without seeing the most famous mainstays: Brezhnev and Honecker kissing by Dmitri Vrubel and Birgit Kinder's Trabant car.

URBAN NATION

Map 5; Bülowstrasse 7, Kreuzberg; ///payer.gossip.meanings;
www.urban-nation.com

Of course the world's first museum devoted to urban art finds itself in
graffiti-obsessed Berlin. This non-profit scoffs at traditional galleries
by turning its walls into endless canvases and, true to the soul of public
art, making admission free. Aspiring street artists come to see local
and international heavyweights – think Banksy and Shepard Fairey.

BOXHAGENER STRASSE

Map 2; Friedrichshain; ///gravest.withdrew.elevated

Street art isn't all big, bold murals (though this street does have some
quirky ones). It's the little details that make a walk along ever-evolving
Boxi such a treat. Look out for quirky posters hidden in doorways, tiny
drawings stencilled on walls and peeling stickers stuck on lampposts.

URBAN SPREE

Map 2; Revaler Strasse 99, Friedrichshain; ///molars.pointed.outsize;
www.urbanspree.com

Most locals would probably swerve off a visit to the touristy RAW-
Gelände complex, where this art centre lies, but the façade is fair
game. Enticing even the most too-cool-for-school locals to drop by is
the gritty "Artist Wall", adorned with abstract pieces that are sprayed
over every month or so from the likes of Zevs, Nychos and 1UP crew.

» Don't leave without visiting the in-house tattooist for a memento
to take home. You're sure to be inspired by the local ink around town.

Liked by the locals

"Berlin is the epicentre of the urban art world, with Urban Nation as the finest platform for street art in the city. It celebrates art in public spaces and the ever-changing face of the capital."

MIA FLORENTINE WEISS, GERMAN CONCEPTUAL
AND PERFORMANCE ARTIST

Cultural Centres

Think of a community centre, and retirees sipping tea on mismatched chairs might come to mind. Not so in Berlin. Here, cool local initiatives invite all walks of life to connect over mutual interests and share stories.

UFAFABRIK

Map 6; Viktoriastrasse 10–18, Tempelhof;
///either.inflict.engaging; www.ufafabrik.de

Back in 1979, locals saved this space from demolition, and began sowing the seeds for the eco-community that flourishes here today. Sustainable living is at the heart of this creative utopia: veggie gardens thrive on the rooftop, an in-house bakery serves up organic bites after strenuous sports lessons, and solar panels generate energy for the concerts, cabaret and dance shows put on here.

KULTURBRAUEREI

Map 1; Schönhauser Allee 36, Prenzlauer Berg;
///friction.aims.hamster; www.kulturbrauerei.de

It's culture, rather than beer, that's brewed up in this 19th-century brewery nowadays (though the beer garden still serves up the good stuff). A social staple for P-Berg dwellers of all kinds, Kulturbrauerei is practically a mini village, its six courtyards and 20 red-and-yellow buildings housing everything you need to never leave. Mums shop for groceries in the morning, retirees take a salsa class in the afternoon and students settle in for open mic events in the evening.

» **Don't leave without** visiting the Museum in der Kulturbrauerei, where a free exhibition showcases everyday life in the GDR.

SILENT GREEN KULTURQUARTIER
Map 6; Gerichtstrasse 35, Wedding; ///cases.civil.whom;
www.silent-green.net

This may have once been a crematorium, but Berliners are breathing new life into it nowadays. A space for research and experimentation, silent green is where start-up folk and music industry heads network over concerts, seminars and shiatsu sessions. Music labels are based here, too, so Nick Cave might just walk past while you're practising your downward dog in a yoga class (his label, !K7 Records, is here).

HAUS DER KULTUREN DER WELT
Map 5; John-Foster-Dulles-Allee 10, Tiergarten;
///fresh.scrum.studio; www.hkw.de

One of the first cultural institutions to open in reunified Berlin, the House of World Cultures is a forward-thinking forum where locals of all backgrounds come together. There's nothing Berliners love more than discussing what the society of tomorrow looks like, or how the arts can help to build a more radical future, and the performances, exhibitions and readings held at HKW aid just that.

Solo, Pair, Crowd

Whether you're keen to meet fellow activists or your mates are craving an intellectual fix, there's a centre to suit.

FLYING SOLO
Get acquainted

Sharehaus Refugio in Neukölln provides far more than housing for refugees. It's easy to make new pals at the café here, with events like language swaps and dancing classes.

IN A PAIR
Culture night

Planning a mate date but can't decide whether to see a film or attend an author reading? Enter ACUD, a funky art house in Mitte where you can do both – and more, like take a vocal workshop or hit up the club.

FOR A CROWD
Get inspired

The more the merrier at Das Baumhaus in Wedding, an indoor "treehouse" bent on knowledge-sharing. Gather your mates and settle on cosy couches to hear a zero-waste talk before a bike-repair workshop begins.

SCHWARTZSCHE VILLA

Map 6; Grunewaldstrasse 55, Steglitz;
///skewed.monopoly.tornado; (030) 902 992 210

This former stately summer house has been a home for all since the 1990s. Artists toil away in the attic atelier, little ones enjoy the small studio theatre, students dart between concerts and etching workshops, and old boys read the newspaper on the summer terrace.

» Don't leave without visiting the café for breakfast. It's run by Mosaik-Services, who support those with disabilities through jobs.

ZK/U

Map 5; Siemensstrasse 27, Moabit; ///galaxies.drank.memo;
www.zku-berlin.org

In this old railway depot, a rotating residency of artists ask how art interacts with – and can change – the urban world we live in. Thought-provoking talks, communal allotments and boules courts draw activists and academics eager to exchange ideas (and have a good time).

OYOUN

Map 3; Lucy-Lameck-Strasse 32, Neukölln;
///treaties.cutback.twin; www.oyoun.de

There's a wonderful spirit of solidarity at this non-profit, where projects from migrant, decolonial and queer feminist perspectives promote discussion. Think plays about the taboos of menstruation, workshops that invite Black trans people to voice their experiences and performances exploring sex work from queer non-binary artists.

An afternoon in
cool Kreuzberg

Back in the 1970s, Kreuzberg made international headlines as a centre of progressive art, radical politics and anti-establishment feeling. This anarchic scene drew squatters, migrants and artists to the area, and inspired the likes of David Bowie and Iggy Pop. Such characters made their mark here but, after the fall of the wall, the area's decadent spirit began to dissipate as gentrification took hold. Still, luxury flats and trendy restaurants aside, many places uphold a revolutionary spirit – if you know where to look.

1. Hansa Studios
Köthener Strasse 38, Kreuzberg; www.hansa studios.de
///rounds.obvious.clan

2. Mehringplatz
Mehringplatz, Kreuzberg
///modern.thankful.educated

3. Südblock
Admiralstrasse 1–2, Kreuzberg; www.sued block.org
///jigging.cautious.busy

4. Kuntsraum Bethanien
Mariannenplatz 2, Kreuzberg; www. kunstraumkreuzberg.de
///arrived.names.fountain

5. SO36
Oranienstrasse 190, Kreuzberg; www.so36.com
///jars.exacted.modules

Checkpoint Charlie
///emails.chairs.brand

Baumhaus an der Mauer
///plotting.plenty.crusher

Soak up history at
HANSA STUDIOS
Book a tour through the famous studios where Bowie recorded his album *Heroes*.

ALEXANDER-
PLATZ

FRIEDRICHSTR

MITTE

GRUNERSTRASSE

Spree

Checkpoint Charlie
*may be the most famous
crossing point between
the East and West, but it's
also a reminder of those
who died fleeing the East.*

ANNENSTRASSE

*In 1983, Turkish
immigrant Osman Kalin
built* **Baumhaus an der
Mauer** *– a treehouse on
a strip of land between
the West and the East.*

Peek around
**KUNTSRAUM
BETHANIEN**

ORANIENSTRASSE

Check out the powerful contemporary
art at this gallery. The building was a
hospital before being repurposed by
squatters and artists in the 1970s.

Check out
MEHRINGPLATZ

Counter-culture lives on
through Kreuzberg's
colourful street art – spot
the most impressive murals
around this plaza.

4

5

Party at
SO36

2

GITSCHINER   STRASSE

3

Pitstop at
SÜDBLOCK

End at this famous club,
the home of punk and
rock music of the 1970s
where the likes of Bowie
and Iggy Pop hit the
dance floor.

KREUZBERG

Stop for a coffee at this
beloved queer bar. It hosts
alternative events, so you
might catch a karaoke
event or cool reading.

KOTTBUSSER DAMM

MEHRINGDAMM

GNEISENAUSTRASSE

HASENHEIDE

NEUKÖLLN

*Volkspark
Hasenheide*

*Flughafen
Tempelhof*

COLUMBIADAMM

0 metres	800
0 yards	800

NIGHTLIFE

Forget New York: Berlin is the city that never sleeps. Whether it's a 72-hour rave or a midnight movie, its nightlife is the rawest expression of Berlin's love for escapism.

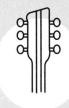

Snack Spots and Spätis

Nights out in Berlin are a marathon, not a sprint. Getting cheap beers from a Späti (convenience store) then grabbing some grub from an Imbiss is standard procedure before hitting a club or gig.

CURRY 36

Map 4; Mehringdamm 36, Kreuzberg; ///aura.shell.floating; www.curry36.de

Occupying the same stretch for four decades, this legendary *Imbiss* serves up some of Berlin's best *Currywurst* to those needing a midnight comfort feed. It's the first port of call for taxi drivers refuelling mid-shift, hedonists energizing before a big night and even the odd celeb wanting to know what all the fuss is about. See for yourself and line your stomach before hitting the next bar.

SPÄTKAUF ROSENBACK

Map 1; Weinbergsweg 27, Mitte; ///driveway.glaze.panthers

The best place to take in the hubbub of Rosenthaler Platz isn't one of its many bars – it's this famed *Späti*. Come evening, its outdoor seating area fills with excitable students sipping Rotkäppchen sparkling wine from paper cups and long-time Berliners guzzling beers from the well-stocked fridge out back. The constant buzz of chatter collides with trams rattling past, sporadically interrupted by a loud guffaw — courtesy of a three-pints-in local.

» Don't leave without finding a seat facing out onto the street to watch life go by while scheming up the night ahead.

AMICI AMICI FOCACCERIA

Map 4; Mehringdamm 42, Kreuzberg; ///softly.awkward.slider; www.amici-amici.de

If anything will keep you going mid-session, it's Italian street food with theatrics to match. You're never quite sure if the boisterous staff are being friendly or pulling your leg here (unless you speak Sicilian), but it's all part of the fun. Italian geezers in puffer jackets watch football on their phones while wobbly boozers point to the delicious fillings they want crammed into their focaccia. Wash it down with a glass of red, poured in Bacchanalian measures by the beaming cashier.

Shh!

It's easy to miss Raamson Liquor *(Gneisenaustrasse 5)*, an unassuming *Späti* with serious street food. As well as stocking a bunch of Asian groceries, this Sri Lankan convenience store dishes up authentic Tamil grub. Take some spicy dumplings out onto the covered tables and tuck in; snacking with beers under the awning is a joy few people know about.

Liked by the locals

"*Spätis* are special simply because they're always there – it's hard to imagine the *Kiez* without them. At Quicky Markt, we're like a living room: we have our regulars, we have a bar, coffee, somewhere to sit outside. It's a beautiful thing."

JENNYFER G,
EMPLOYEE AT QUICKY MARKT SPÄTI & BAR

QUICKY MARKT SPÄTI & BAR

Map 2; Skalitzer Strasse 96, Kreuzberg; ///riper.degree.axed

This much-loved *Späti* epitomizes Kreuzberg's community spirit. The vibe here is familial, where owners always welcome you with a smile, whether you've been coming for years or you're new in town. Outside, weathered punks hang around reminiscing, sipping budget beers and mixing with a younger pre-club crew. A home away from home.

IMREN

Map 3; Karl-Marx-Strasse 75, Neukölln; ///protest.damage.saves

The D in Berlin's DNA could very well stand for döner. It's a myth that it was born here, but the Berlin style – juicy meat in toasted flatbread – is a city original. And Imren does one of the best in town. The *Yaprak* kebab consists of thin strips of beef and lamb fat stacked on a vertical spit; seeing this beefy behemoth rotate in Imren's window mid-session is almost as mesmeric as the meaty greatness of the kebabs it yields.

» **Don't leave without** ordering a *dürüm* if you've got a munch on, or grab a pide as an extra side to share. It's all so good.

BASMAH

Map 3; Reichenberger Strasse 26, Kreuzberg; ///haggis.foil.split;
www.basmah-berlin.de

Eating a messy sandwich sober is a challenge here, let alone a few drinks in. But wiping insanely tasty peanut sauce from your chin every two seconds is a small price to pay for these Sudanese pittas, packed with crispy falafel, deep-fried halloumi and crunchy salad.

Cool Clubs

Berlin's always done hedonism well, and nothing speaks to that more than its mind-altering clubs. Expect the post-wall spirit, with locals high on freedom and raving it up well into Monday morning.

ZUR KLAPPE

Map 4; Yorckstrasse 2, Kreuzberg; ///decorate.connects.complains;
www.zurklappe.org

Look for the staircase in Yorckstrasse's middle boulevard and knock – getting into this tiny underground club is as simple as that. Housed in an old U-Bahn station toilet, it garners its name from its heyday as a gay cruising spot (known as a *Klappe*). These days, sweaty bodies move to techno around sewage pipes and graffitied tiles. The sound quality is a mess, but the high-frequency energy makes up for it.

://ABOUT BLANK

Map 2; Markgrafendamm 24, Friedrichshain;
///handed.starter.winner; www.aboutblank.li

The no-frills parties at this former illegal rave den are famously down and dirty. Sweat and smoke intermingle while regulars pack out sticky dance floors – one pumping out hard techno, the other

The golden rules of getting in here are knowing the DJ line-ups (you might be quizzed) and waiting.

deep house, most likely. When the heat inside gets too much, come up for air in the backyard, where 72-hour raves play out in the summer.

SALON ZUR WILDEN RENATE

Map 2; Alt-Stralau 70, Friedrichshain;
///wash.successor.unusually; www.renate.cc

This old tenement block hosts the loosest parties, harking back to 1990s East Berlin when carefree clubbers raved it up in empty apartments. You'll get disorientated in its labyrinth-like warren of dance floors — decked out with lava lamps, sofas and quirky art — and emerge blinking into the sunlight with no clue what day it is.

» Don't leave without snapping a picture in the photobooth, for a reminder of what you looked like after a night dancing to trippy disco.

BEATE UWE

Map 1; Schillingstrasse 31, Mitte; ///cascade.gates.safest; www.beate-uwe.de

It's easy to miss this tiny gem. Nestled between dated GDR apartment blocks, Beate Uwe's nondescript exterior looks more like a community centre than a club. But appearances are deceiving in this city. Inside, everyone seems to know each other (okay, it kind of feels like a community centre), embracing like old friends to the chugging beat of downtempo electro and Italo disco, obligatory G&Ts in hand. If you're still going come Sunday, pop down for cosy afterparty vibes and a mint tea on the carpet-covered dance floor.

OHM

Map 4; Köpenicker Strasse 70, Kreuzberg; ///nest.crass.mocking; www.ohmberlin.com

While technoheads queue for famed club Tresor, those in the know slink past to its tiny underground neighbour. Housed in the battery room of a defunct power plant, OHM is an intimate haunt for purists, where transcendence is found through avant-garde electronic music.

BERGHAIN

Map 2; Am Wriezener Bahnhof, Friedrichshain; ///period.talkers.crystals; www.berghain.berlin

If there's any club that people are willing to queue three hours for only to risk a stern head shake at the door, it's Berghain. A badass techno temple in a former power station, Berlin's most illustrious nightclub has just as much a reputation for its world-class DJs and sound system as its notorious door policy. Our advice? Wear black, don't speak English, know the DJ lineup and, well, just try

Shh!

Apart from a cryptic website and a few red herrings, the hidden club Heideglühen (*Seestrasse 1*) in Wedding has little online trace. Finding it is intentionally hard, and your chances of getting in are slim — unless you bring a mate who's been before, and dress to dance. Saturday mornings attract seasoned ravers, so try your luck then.

your luck – if the bouncer lets you in, you'll enter a phantasmagoria of thumping bass and flesh-baring fashion. Mooch around industrial mazes, eye up weird art, take a break in the elusive gelato bar and – if you're up for it – enter the darkroom where strangers get acquainted. What happens in Berghain stays here.

>> Don't leave without ordering a drink from Panorama Bar upstairs and waiting for the window blinds to flash open after sunrise.

KITKAT CLUB

Map 4; Köpenicker Strasse 76, Mitte; ///claim.type.acre; www.kitkatclub.org

This is more than just a sex club – it's divine decadence. Racy, way over-the-top outfits (or, no outfits at all) are the uniform here, where a sea of latex, leather, glitter and PVC gear fills a packed dance floor. Watchful bouncers, a phone ban and open-minded punters keep the space very safe and respectful, and there's no pressure to do anything other than dance whimsically to techno and house beats.

MS HOPPETOSSE

Map 2; Eichenstrasse 4, Alt-Treptow; ///lighten.toasted.sampled; www.hoppetosse.berlin

Moored up on the Spree, this old pleasure craft is a club circuit classic. During summer, friendly faces drink on the top deck before heading down below for the evening's odyssey. The music carries on pumping as night turns to day through the portholes; come morning, wavy ravers bob about to house and techno tunes, sunglasses firmly on.

Live Music

Music is Berlin's lifeblood, but it's not all techno DJ sets here. Sure, monotonous beats have their place, but bold vocals, sultry saxophone tones and gentle guitar strums make for equally unforgettable nights.

MADAME CLAUDE

Map 2; Lübbener Strasse 19, Kreuzberg;
///outlast.bumpy.beaker; www.madameclaude.de

No, you haven't had one too many shots – there really are chairs on the ceiling here. Combining a trippy, red-room aesthetic with retro furnishings, this underground rock venue has the vibe of your mate's party (if their house was upside down). Simply rock up to enjoy a gig, then pull up a chair (those on the floor, that is) to chill out post-show.

Try it!
BE OPEN

Love the surprise of open mic nights? Check out Prachtwerk *(www.pracht werkberlin.com)* on a Wednesday night to hear undiscovered sounds – or better yet, email ahead for a performance slot.

SO36

Map 3; Oranienstrasse 190, Kreuzberg; ///jars.exacted.modules;
www.so36.com

The mother of Berlin's punk movement, SO36's claim to fame as the
CBGB (NYC's iconic music club) of Europe reached fever pitch in the
1970s, when David Bowie and Iggy Pop partied here. Though it's more
raved about for its club nights, the live rock and metal gigs are as
vibrant as ever. Pre-book to breathe in the palpable sense of history.

BI NUU

Map 2; U-Bahnhof Schlesisches Tor, Kreuzberg;
///void.ships.maternal; www.binuu.de

Grown-up scenesters, beer-soaked and shiny with perspiration, jump
to the sounds of rising rock, folk and electro bands in this scruffy spot.
With cracked paintwork and the muggy scent of sweat, it's got all the
hallmarks of the venues you worshipped as a teenager, minus the angst.

ZIG ZAG

Map 5; Hauptstrasse 89, Schöneberg; ///stoops.that.entry;
www.zigzag-jazzclub.berlin

This cosy jazz club has always been about building a base of loyal
regulars – just look to the suave set who chat like old friends between
a rotating roster of jazz, funk and soul acts. You can just turn up, but
save the defeat of not nabbing a candlelit table and book ahead.

» Don't leave without donating. There's no entry fee; rather, you pay
what you wish into a collection at the end of a show.

Solo, Pair, Crowd

Berlin bangs the drum for every genre imaginable, and whatever your tempo, there's something for everyone.

FLYING SOLO
Get moshed
Dig out the battered Converses and get down to Wild at Heart, a tiki-style dive bar in Kreuzberg famous for its punk and rock 'n' roll gigs.

IN A PAIR
Hold (jazz) hands
For a Sunday brunch date with a smooth side of jazz, head to Yorckschlösschen, a romantic *Traditionskneipe* (traditional pub) in Kreuzberg that's been hitting the right notes for 120 years.

FOR A CROWD
Analogue vibes
Nights out with pals at Wedding's Panke Culture go beyond the well-trodden techno trope. Start in the beer garden then head indoors for live reggae and bouncy hip hop vibes.

MUSIKBRAUEREI

Map 1; Am Schweizer Garten 82–4, Prenzlauer Berg;
///recently.watched.novelist; www.musikbrauerei.com

Friends tell friends, who tell yet more friends, about this tumbledown brewery, one of the scene's most whispered-about secrets. Inside, a wine-quaffing crowd huddle on chairs around a small stage, awaiting gigs from avant-garde acts spanning electronic, folk and classical. As soon as they start, a hush descends and an intimate night begins.

FUNKHAUS

Map 6; Nalepastrasse 18, Oberschöneweide; ///evening.fall.gain;
www.funkhaus-berlin.net

There's always a pulse-quickening moment when you get tickets to a Funkhaus concert. Built to be East Germany's radio HQ, this futuristic studio complex is idolized for its world-class acoustics – something the electronic and indie acts who play here praise.

» Don't leave without having a pre-gig snack and beer in Milchbar, the building's former canteen with views of the Spree.

THE HAT

Map 5; Lotte-Lenya-Bogen 550, Charlottenburg;
///headed.mailer.prowess; www.thehatbar.de

This railway arch jazz bar is a far cry from the stuffiness of the city's more established venues. After work, Charlottenburgers trickle into its tunnel-like interior and prop up the long wooden bar, casually slugging whisky and waiting for talented musicians to jam.

LGBTQ+ Scene

Ever since claiming its crown as Europe's gay capital in the 1920s, Berlin's LGBTQ+ scene has been effervescent. Whether you're dreaming of the ultra-risqué or the mega-mellow, there's a night for all tastes.

ROSES

Map 3; Oranienstrasse 187, Kreuzberg; ///adopt.dashes.offshore

Everyone's had a night to remember at Roses. Berlin's ultimate bad-decision gay bar, this pink fuzzy-walled joint is the place you end up at after other bars have closed, taking cheap Mexikaner (tequila and tabasco) shots, flirting with a stranger under the disco ball and heading off to that newfound friend's afterparty at sunrise.

NEUES UFER

Map 5; Hauptstrasse 157, Schöneberg; ///rice.town.evoked; (030) 7895 7900

What do David Bowie's Berlin years and LGBTQ+ history have in common? Everything at this Schöneberg institution. Opened in 1977, New Shore (originally called Anderes Ufer, or Other Shore) was Germany's first openly gay and lesbian café, its uncurtained windows symbolizing a will to be seen to the world. Bowie, who lived a few doors down, often popped in, and posters here are a homage to this popular patron. Berlin's kings and queens continue to live like heroes at this original hangout today, even if just for a few casual beers to start the night off right.

SÜDBLOCK

Map 3; Admiralstrasse 1–2, Kreuzberg; ///jigging.cautious.busy; www.suedblock.org

A queer pub with the relaxed vibes of a traditional German beer garden, Südblock is where those ultimate easy-going summer nights unfold. When you're not snacking on *Currywurst*, sipping cheap beer and chatting with cute bears at the next table, get involved in the donation-based events. Plucky drag shows, poetry readings and quiz nights, as well as counselling services, make this an important place for both the LGBTQ+ community and local residents.

» Don't leave without booking in for the affordable Sunday brunch, a cult favourite that tends to be a boozy all-day affair.

SCHWUZ

Map 3; Rollbergstrasse 26, Neukölln; ///smarter.pile.fine; www.schwuz.de

This is Berlin's go-to gay club for nights of sweaty dancing. The fun-loving crowd – mostly fashion-forward fellas, but also genderqueer folks and allies – are always up for partying all night long to pop, indie, hip hop and techno tunes. Hands-in-the-air boogying on several dance floors aside, SchwuZ also hosts drag queens, film screenings, literary readings and, above all, a welcoming space to gossip over a coffee – check the website for all its upcoming mischief.

CHANTALS HOUSE OF SHAME

Map 2; Suicide Circus, RAW Gelände, Revaler Strasse 99, Friedrichshain; ///crowned.prices.landmark; www.house-of-shame.com

Helmed by local drag legend Chantal, this kooky gay party has been a Thursday night institution for over two decades. Drawing in a vibrant pastiche of drag queens, queer men, allies and even celebs (Katy Perry has partied here) are camp numbers from Chantal and her merry band of performers, cheesy pop and electro tracks, and all the sequined smocks you could wish for. Nights out don't get more silly, upbeat and in your face than this.

SILVER FUTURE

Map 3; Weserstrasse 206, Neukölln; ///snipe.sulky.horn; www.silverfuture.net

Rainbow flags hung proudly in the window and a cheeky sign behind the bar declaring "you just left the heteronormative sector" sum up kitschy Silver Future. Come with the right attitude (no nonsense, please) to this provocative lesbian hangout and bubbly locals welcome you warmly. Expect to leave with new best friends after spending hours chatting to the folks on the table beside you.

PORNCEPTUAL

Map 1; Alte Münze, Molkenmarkt 2, Mitte; ///random.articulated.snores; www.pornceptual.com

Kinky clubbers never skip Pornceptual's monthly sex parties, firm fixtures in the queer clubbing calendar. What started as an online platform championing ethical porn swiftly turned into sex- and body-positive club nights, providing a safe, inclusive space for hedonism. The crowd is cool, diverse and down to experiment, and an anything-goes yet respectful abandon makes nights here unforgettable. Leave your inhibitions – and clothes – at the door (showing some flesh gets you cut-price entry), and bring an open mind.

MONSTER RONSON'S ICHIBAN KARAOKE

Map 2; Warschauer Strasse 34, Friedrichshain; ///points.divided.shirt; www.karaokemonster.de

Anyone can – and, boy, do they attempt to – become a pop star diva beneath the swirling disco balls at this institution. It's always packed out at the weekends, when a mixed crew belt out their best Britney cover and soak up the applause, spurred on by ample glasses of wine. Things barely simmer down on school nights, with Tuesday shows hosted by Berlin drag hero Pansy and *Drag Race* screenings.

» Don't leave without trying to score a private cabin – perfect if you're mic shy or with a small group. Your best bet is booking ahead.

Try it!
TWIRL SOME TASSELS

Amp up the fun and take a burlesque class at Prenzlauer Berg's famous Berlin Burlesque Academy *(www.berlin-burlesque-academy.com)*, where you'll learn about the fabulous art of performing.

Nights by the Water

For all its concrete and brick, Berlin is shaped around water – and so are Berliners' nights. When days get longer, Berliners live it up in open-air riverside clubs, on bridges above the canals and at pop-up beach bars.

ADMIRALBRÜCKE

Map 3; Admiralstrasse, Kreuzberg; ///stereos.hands.flames

The din of evening revellers can be heard up the street as you approach this infamous cobblestone bridge on the Landwehrkanal, where a street party vibe prevails in the summer. Pals meeting after work, couples en route to date nights and students breaking from study sessions pitch up on the pavement with *Späti*-bought beers

Shh!

Torfstrassensteg, a narrow footbridge in Moabit, is one of those spots you could pass a thousand times and not even blink an eye. Not so for those-in-the-know, who come here to savour one of Berlin's most mesmeric sunsets. As the day fades, beer bottles clink as the nearby power plant pulses in an orangey glow, the canal below shimmering.

and pizzas, worshipping the evening sun while buskers strum their guitars. Once they've seen the day out, everyone tends to drift off to a bar to continue the weekend (or home, if it's a school night).

CLUB DER VISIONAERE

Map 2; Am Flutgraben, Kreuzberg; ///panels.wipes.investor; www.clubdervisionaere.com

Summer officially starts for Berlin's party kids when CDV, as it's known, opens. Split between a small brick building and a wooden pontoon jutting out into the canal, it's a club more famous for its sultry after-hours vibes than marathon raves. Well-known DJs play out from a booth on the building's ground floor while mellow clubbers sway lazily on the covered dance floor, or chill under a partially scorched weeping willow that shades part of the deck.

YAAM

Map 2; An der Schillingbrücke 3, Friedrichshain; ///suitable.ground.shady; www.yaam.de

Since opening in 1994, the Young African Arts Market has been a cornerstone of Berlin subculture. Leisurely hours pass by here as all walks of life soak up sunshiny Afro-Caribbean vibes beside the Spree. Days are reserved for chilling barefoot in the sand at the beach bar, munching jerk chicken and sipping chilled beers. Come night, a shack-like club bustles with reggae, dancehall and afrobeat tunes.

» **Don't leave without** trying a banana beer, a YAAM summer classic. It's not as weird as it sounds, and you'll be hooked after one.

ELSE

Map 2; An den Treptowers 10, Alt-Treptow;
///eternity.dramatic.capers; www.else.tv

It's all about the Sunday sessions at this open-air riverside hangout,
run by the crew behind Salon Zur Wilden Renate *(p145)*. Colourful
shipping containers frame the dance floor decking, where daytime
ravers and the straight-through crew groove it out to renowned DJs,
not one soul worried about Monday.

» Don't leave without catching a moment on a covered deckchair
up on the terrace and gazing out to the shimmering Spree.

CAMILA-UFER/BOULEPLATZ

Map 3; Paul-Lincke-Ufer 13, Kreuzberg; ///punk.require.perfume

Pétanque is the name of the game at this bankside square, where dab
hands and upstarts jostle competitively, arguing over the last throw
and cheering when things go their way. Beers are *de rigueur*, though
you'll probably clock the odd bottle of pastis being swigged by a crafty
old boy. Nab a bench facing the thoroughfare to people-watch.

DREILÄNDERECK

Map 3; Lohmühlenstrasse 37, Alt-Treptow; ///shiny.barman.sung

The canalside confluence where Kreuzberg, Neukölln and Treptow
meet is prime summer sundowner territory. Adventurous locals take to
the waterways to form a festive flotilla of inflatable dinghies, pumping
out a cacophony of tunes from portable speakers – you might even
catch the odd band arrive by boat, drop anchor and perform on the

 When you get peckish, grab a pie to-go from W Pizza, a popular Neapolitan on nearby Weichselplatz.

water. Hours go missing in this boozy Bermuda Triangle, and as the daylight fades it's on to someone's flat to prep for the night ahead. Dreamy stuff.

MONBIJOU-UFER

Map 1; Oranienburger Strasse, Mitte; ///shifting.dolphin.siesta

Riverside revelry beside a UNESCO World Heritage site goes down a treat at this little promenade, located on Monbijou Park's southern flank. Gaggles of mates spend balmy evenings here, admiring the revivalist architecture of Museum Island across the Spree while catching up on the day's antics. Laughter and chatter mix in the sticky summer air, punctuated by the occasional prosecco cork popping free.

HOLZMARKT

Map 2; Holzmarktstrasse 25, Friedrichshain; ///staples.parrot.traps;
www.holzmarkt.com

In 2008, passionate locals voted to save this stretch of riverbank from becoming another soulless development. Much to the relief of heartbroken ravers, the former site of legendary Bar 25 was instead to become a sustainable urban village – still with a club, the quirky Kater Blau. Everyone's welcome in this alternative community, from project-planning creatives after a workspace to green-fingered families tending its city farm. As evening approaches, onlookers soak up the DIY carnival buzz from wooden benches and hammocks, sipping their BYO beers and discussing the day gone by.

Classic Cinemas

*Evenings in Berlin are not all high energy. Night owls
find refuge in indie cinemas and historic theatres,
where arthouse flicks, themed showings and
throwback classics feed eclectic interests.*

FREILUFTKINO FRIEDRICHSHAIN

**Map 6; Landsberger Allee 15, Friedrichshain; ///property.causes.editor;
www.freiluftkino-berlin.de**

As soon as summer hits the city, everyone scrambles to book tickets to
the outdoor screenings *(p9)* that take over Berlin. Those in the middle
of Volkspark Friedrichshain, an art gallery's courtyard, are the biggest
– and most idyllic. Classics and last season favourites entertain a
laidback crowd who don't really mind what they view; instead, it's all
about cuddling up on benches under the stars on a balmy night.

ROLLBERG KINOS

**Map 3; Rollbergstrasse 70, Neukölln; ///feeds.messed.savings;
www.yorck.de/kinos/rollberg**

When mates trek through the shabby Rollberg mall, it's not bargains
they're hunting for – it's this small cinema, showing one of Berlin's
biggest selections of indie movies in the original language version.

Most movies in Berlin are dubbed, so pick a screening marked OV (original version) or OMEU (with English subtitles).

Saturday nights see them all swapping club sweats for cinema scares, when the Creepy Crypt horror special shows gory classics and new releases. (Tip: the chairs recline, if it all gets too much.)

SPUTNIK

Map 4; Hasenheide 54, Neukölln; ///tens.oath.fellow; www.sputnik-kino.com

Hiding high up in a nondescript office building, Sputnik feels like a cinema in a squat. Inside, loyal regulars swarm the cluttered box office, vying for tickets to the latest Hollywood or indie flick. When the credits roll, they move to the cosy drawing room, smoking on the balcony and discussing the merits of the film by the makeshift bar.

» Don't leave without seeing a flick in Theatre 1, where the front row is uniquely stone-built. There are two-seater chairs for couples, too.

BABYLON

Map 1; Rosa-Luxemburg-Strasse 30, Mitte; ///proof.basin.removing; www.babylonberlin.eu

Catching a flick at this 1920s city landmark (so iconic, it inspired a Netflix series of the same name) feels like a throwback to the movie-going golden era. Every Saturday at midnight, old souls settle in for free silent movies, accompanied by an organist in the restored orchestra pit. The rest of the week, this Art Deco beauty is ground zero for German and international arthouse. It's a delightful far cry from commercial theatres.

Solo, Pair, Crowd

Whether you've got a few hours to yourself or are craving a night out with a cinematic twist, Berlin's film landscape has you covered.

FLYING SOLO
Hog the armrest
A tiny cinema with the feel of a living room, the indie Lichtblick Kino in Prenzlauer Berg is the perfect place to cosy up and take in a political documentary without your friend whispering away beside you.

IN A PAIR
Mate date
Watch life unfold with a drink on Neukölln's popular Weserstrasse before heading into Wolf, an intimate arthouse cinema, for a carefully selected indie flick.

FOR A CROWD
Get quiz-ical
If you and your mates spend hours watching films together (so you know all the lines to *The Avengers* and who won that Oscar in 2003), put your knowledge to the test at SO36's *(p149)* occasional film quiz.

KINO CENTRAL

**Map 1; Rosenthaler Strasse 39, Mitte; ///laying.lamps.outlast;
www.kino-central.de**

This pint-sized theatre is as cool as they come, hidden in the back of street art mecca Haus Schwarzenberg *(p129)*. It gets packed (watch your elbows), but you'll feel at home on comfy seats with a beer in hand. In the summer, screenings migrate to the (still small) courtyard.

» Don't leave without having a drink at Café Cinema, a bohemian bar in the courtyard filled with silver-screen memorabilia.

ASTOR FILMLOUNGE

**Map 5; Kurfürstendamm 225, Charlottenburg; ///shutting.tonsils.given;
www.berlin.premiumkino.de**

Formerly known as the Kiki, the Astor Filmlounge has been the go-to spot for classy date nights since 1948. While the name has changed, the mid-century glamour has remained: valet parking, champagne on arrival, a cloakroom, reclinable leather seats and even a red carpet. The films, much like the experience, are typical Hollywood.

KINO INTERNATIONAL

**Map 1; Karl-Marx-Allee 33, Friedrichshain; ///shaky.parting.images;
www.kino-international.com**

Back in the 1960s, Kino International was where (mostly) socialist films in the GDR premiered. The programme is much more varied today – think cool indie screenings, big soirees during Berlinale's film festival season, and MonGay, a beloved night of LGBTQ+ films.

0 metres 200

0 yards 200

Volkspark Hasenheide

COLUMBIADAMM

FLUGHAFENSTRASSE

FONTANESTRASSE

HERMANNSTRASSE

Snack at
LIBANON FALAFEL
Take a pit stop to enjoy some authentic shawarma and falafel, all for €1.50 a pop.

3

Sip a cocktail at
KEITH BAR
Cheers to the night with a whiskey sour at this rustic bar, which specializes in world-class whiskeys.

2

A popular spot to meet for beers, **Herrfurthplatz** *is home to a spire-less church today after it was deemed a hazard for landing aircraft.*

Watch the sunset at
TEMPELHOFER FELD
Find a patch of grass, play some tunes on your phone and watch as day turns to night.

1 HERRFURTHSTRASSE

LICHENRADER STRASSE

SCHILLERPROMENADE

WEISESTRASSE

KIENITZER STRASSE

5

Rave it up at
PROMENADEN ECK
Head to this bar/club in the early hours to move to DJ-spun tunes. There are also ample sofas, should you need a break from dancing.

4

Sway to sounds at
SOWIESO NEUKÖLLN E.V.
Try for a table at this jazz bar; the Dutch painter at its helm curates a top-notch roster of acts, so you're in for a treat.

The sail-like pavillion at Tempelhof's community garden **Allmende Kontor** *sometimes hosts sunset concerts and festivals.*

Anita-Berber-Park

A night out in
buzzy Schillerkiez

When it comes to a night out, oh-so-trendy Neukölln is where it's at. The lively strip of bars along Weserstrasse may get all the attention, but the real fun lies in the little micro-hood of Schillerkiez. Low-flying jets, courtesy of former airport Tempelhof, meant this 'hood was once quite shabby, but today young creatives brighten the area. The best nights out in Berlin tend to follow the same route: great grub, live music, dancing into the morning. Schillerkiez has it all.

1. Tempelhofer Feld
Tempelhofer
Damm, Tempelhof
///widget.hillside.caring

2. Keith Bar
Schillerpromenade 2,
Neukölln; www.keith
barberlin.de
///down.fragment.bleach

3. Libanon Falafel
Flughafenstrasse 34, Neukölln
///engages.jaunts.exhaled

4. Sowieso Neukölln e.V.
Weisestrasse 24, Neukölln;
www.sowieso-neukoelln.de
///pine.examiner.humid

5. Promenaden Eck
Schillerpromenade 11,
Neukölln; 0162 694 1825
///quickly.coupler.feeds

Herrfurthplatz ///social.ejects.upholds

Allmende Kontor ///partner.spends.trim

OUTDOORS

Don't believe Berlin's reputation as a grey metropolis. In reality, endless green spaces, scenic lakes and lush urban gardens breathe colour and calm into the hectic city.

Green Spaces

For such an urban city, Berlin is surprisingly green – something that locals don't take for granted, using these open spaces to picnic with pals, top up tans or perfect a skateboard trick.

PARK AM GLEISDREIECK

**Map 4; entrance at Möckernstrasse 26, Kreuzberg;
///teach.kinder.pans; (030) 700 906 710**

Built on the site of a former rail freight wasteland, this modern park still retains emblems of its past, with rusty tracks blending with green lawns and playgrounds. Though train tracks still run through it, it's no longer about the journey here. Rather, this park is the ultimate leisure destination for Kreuzbergers. Come the weekend, boarders pack out the skatepark, families enjoy birthday picnics on the grass and beekeeping locals natter at the intercultural community garden.

GÖRLITZER PARK

Map 2; entrance at Görlitzer Strasse 3, Kreuzberg; ///gain.steers.lunging

It's all a bit anarchic at Görli, a microcosm of Kreuzberg's alternative scene. Every day is a party in the summer, when crowds are drawn like magnets to the giant crater in the centre. A haze of smoke and

 Visit on May Day, when techno pumps out from mobile rigs and street vendors mix cut-price cocktails. drumbeats fill the air while hippies play footbag, mates launch frisbees and Turkish families host epic BBQs. It's loud, messy and not for the fainthearted.

TEMPELHOFER FELD

Map 4; entrance at Tempelhofer Damm, Tempelhof;
///widget.hillside.caring

The Feld is the ultimate symbol of Berlin's fierce community spirit. Nowhere else would a disused airfield be transformed into a huge park rather than a sea of flats after public vote, but that's Berliners for you. And the old runways and surrounding heathland have justifiably become their communal backyard. Where planes once taxied, skaters, cyclists and rollerbladers jet by, passing soloists idling on the grass, groups grilling up a storm and kites dancing in the sky above.

VOLKSPARK HUMBOLDTHAIN

Map 1; entrance at Brunnenstrasse, Gesundbrunnen, Wedding;
///catch.passage.aims

As soon as the sun rises, adrenaline junkies bolt to this beloved adventure playground, scaling concrete edifices and bombing it down the toboggan run built on piled up-rubble. For the non-early risers, the park becomes an afternoon escape, where time is spent wandering the pretty rose garden and strolling under the pergolas.
» Don't leave without climbing up to the viewing platform atop the World War II flak tower for some of the best views over the city.

TREPTOWER PARK

Map 6; entrance at Puschkinallee, Alt-Treptow; ///feared.catch.tingled

When friends agree to gather for a picnic, this Spree-side park is always thrown into the mix. Mammoth summertime feasts are standard on the lawns near the imposing Soviet war memorial, but head out to the *Karpfenteich* (carp pond), a secluded little lake, and idyllic holiday vibes await. Doe-eyed lovers watch boats sail past and bronzed locals top up their tans between beer sips.

TIERGARTEN

Map 5; entrance via Strasse des 17. Juni, Tiergarten; ///crown.painters.after

The emerald in Berlin's crown, Tiergarten is to Berliners what Central Park is to New Yorkers: a favourite meeting place, a people's park and the heart of the community. Once the royal hunting grounds for the Elector of Brandenburg, it's now the stomping ground of joggers and cyclists who use the paths to blow off steam and 9-to-5ers detaching from city life in its picturesque meadows. It's massive, and

Shh!

Ivy-covered façades, beautiful balustrades and stepped fountains in gritty Neukölln? You heard it right. The little Körnerpark *(Schierker Strasse 8)* is a haven from the smoggy clang of Hermannstrasse, and sufficiently off-piste to elude the crowds. Clued-up locals spend their afternoons lazing on the well-kept lawns (even if it's technically verboten).

you need a whole day to explore properly, but if you've only got a few hours, come for an evening stroll – the gaslit footpaths give it an atmosphere like nowhere else, especially in early autumn.

» **Don't leave without** visiting the poignant Memorial to Homosexuals Persecuted under Nazism on the park's eastern fringe.

GÄRTEN DER WELT

Map 6; entrance at Blumberger Damm 44, Marzahn;
///salsa.drill.uptake; www.gaertenderwelt.de

Let's be honest, unless you're into brutalist architecture, you're probably going to consider Marzahn a dull district. But skipping it would mean missing the Gardens of the World, which is anything but boring. This is where parents rock their babies to sleep while meandering nine internationally themed gardens, retirees indulge in tea ceremonies in Chinese tea houses and fresh-faced lovers get married among Balinese temples and Japanese pagodas. If anything gives Marzahn residents a reason to shout "we live here!", it's this tranquil spot.

VIKTORIAPARK

Map 4; entrance via Kreuzbergstrasse, Kreuzberg; ///crisp.joggers.codes

In a city flat as a pancake, Viktoriapark is a welcome anomaly. Set atop an ancient moraine, it's home to a towering Prussian war memorial – the cross on top giving Kreuzberg, literally "Cross Hill", its name. While parents dip their feet and kids splash about in the artificial waterfall, young Kreuzbergers head to the slopes to laze about, toasting the sunset over Berlin as dusk falls.

Community Gardens and Urban Farms

Eco-conscious Berliners (that is, 99 per cent of locals) are all for locally grown produce and a greener city. Enter trending urban gardens, where all walks of life come to connect with nature – and one another.

HIMMELBEET

Map 6; Ruheplatzstrasse 12, Wedding; ///usages.jogging.spends; www.himmelbeet.de

"Solidarity can change everything," or so says the sign at this community garden. And the regular Wedding residents that use the space would testify to that, too. A good life for everyone is the goal here, and no matter who you are, himmelbeet welcomes and inspires you to make a change – be it through a workshop on horticulture, an event on sustainable living or simply the opportunity to lease a communal area and begin harvesting your own produce. The community vibes are palpable, so stop by for a natter while friends and families tend to their tomatoes and mint plants.

» Don't leave without trying the farm-to-fork cuisine in the garden café, where the home-grown vegetables are turned into fantastic low-waste dishes – all vegan, naturally.

PRINZESSINNENGÄRTEN

Map 4; Prinzenstrasse 35–8, Moritzplatz, Kreuzberg;
///frocks.snow.cake; www.prinzessinnengarten.net

Built by and for the locals, trendy Princess Gardens is all about knowledge-sharing. If the eco-conscious volunteers don't already have the answer to your query, a workshop will – think topics like DIY cultivation, permaculture, fermentation and worm composting. Come for lunch in the outdoor café to taste the fruits of their labour and you'll be asking for the public gardening times before you know it.

GARTEN DER HOFFNUNG

Map 6; c/o IB-Übergangswohnheim, Alfred-Randt-Strasse 19, Köpenick;
///misted.options.shift; www.garten-der-hoffnung.net

To aid intercultural exchange at a refugee home, two local women started the Garden of Hope. It's done the trick. Not only do residents jointly take care of the veggies, they also come together to practise language skills and exchange recipes. Interested gardeners are free to join; pop by on a Friday afternoon to mingle over coffee.

Try it!
GUERRILLA GARDENING

Leave no trace – except for a seed bomb. Purchase little clay balls of plant seeds from Seedbomb City *(www.seedbomb.city)*, throw them into your chosen patch of greenery and pop back to see how big they get.

Liked by the locals

"In a city full of apartment dwellers, Berlin's community-driven green spaces are a welcome change of scenery: a chance to get outside, feel the soil between your fingers and reconnect with nature."

MELISA GRAY-WARD, WRITER AND CLIMATE PODCASTER

GEMEINSCHAFTSGARTEN NEUE GRÜNSTRASSE

Map 4; Neue Grünstrasse 13, Mitte; ///siblings.class.workshops; www.pflanz-was.vattenfall.de

Energy supplier Vattenfall's creatively themed space will have you rethinking what a community garden can be. Littl'uns fill wellies with soil, students sprinkle flower seeds in bicycle baskets and parents plant herbs in saucepans – and it's all delightfully free.

» Don't leave without taking a well-deserved break in the relaxation corner, where sun loungers and parasols are up for grabs.

ALLMENDE KONTOR

Map 4; Tempelhofer Feld, Neukölln; ///partner.spends.trim; www.allmende-kontor.de

In the midst of all the rollerbladers at Tempelhofer Feld *(p169)*, green-fingered locals roll up their sleeves and get dirty. This urban garden isn't prettified (suitcases and basketballs are planters), but it's a dreamy spot to just sit between beds of Swiss chard and enjoy the sun.

HORSTWIRTSCHAFT

Map 3; Karl-Marx-Strasse 66, Neukölln; ///gliders.tailed.sobered; www.horstwirtschaft.de

Nothing says Berlin like a community garden nestled in a rooftop bar. Visit during the week and you'll join a post-work crowd of creatives and techies growing some kale, downing tools only to sip an Aperol Spritz and jam to tunes, courtesy of an in-house DJ.

Swimming Spots

Berliners love a dip – heck, some even like a skinny dip, known here as FKK (free body culture, or naturism). When the first signs of spring arrive, it's straight to a lake or lido to cool down.

SCHLACHTENSEE

Map 6; Am Schlachtensee, Zehlendorf; ///fizzled.tags.span

Every Berliner has their favourite lake, and for the students at the nearby Freie Universität, Schlachtensee is unbeatable. Time seems to stretch here, a bit like those long teenage summers you can just about remember. Buddies sunbathe on the grass, adjusting their sunglasses to watch post-exam revellers rope swing into the city's cleanest lake. Once the sun goes in, follow the crowds to the Fischerhütte restaurant on the banks of the lake for a Radler, Germany's answer to shandy.

SOMMERBAD NEUKÖLLN

Map 4; Columbiadamm 160, Neukölln; ///paddle.garages.works;
www.berlinerbaeder.de

Expect nothing but classic poolside scenes at this local lido, where the sounds of excited shouts and splashing water combine with the smell of freshly fried chips. Parents dash after excited tots and kidults

For some peace and quiet, head to Berlin's beloved Vabali spa and recline in the outdoor pool after hitting the saunas.

lark about on the waterslides while burly lifeguards shout orders over a booming loudspeaker. Feeling brazen? Join the queue of fearless kids waiting to catapult from the 10-metre diving board.

SOMMERBAD KREUZBERG

Map 4; Prinzenstrasse 113–9, Kreuzberg; ///evidently.lifts.prestige; www.berlinerbaeder.de

Utterly rammed at the weekend with excitable kids, happy mates and the odd medallion man lording it up, Sommerbad Kreuzberg is a different story during the week. Prise yourself out of bed before 8am and you'll get reduced entry and a calmer pool, filled only with a pre-work crowd getting their lengths in.

» Don't leave without grabbing a well-earned coffee and croissant from the café after your swim. Carpe diem, so they say.

SOMMERBAD OLYMPIASTADION

Map 6; Olympischer Platz 3, Charlottenburg; ///vehicle.toolbar.herring; www.berlinerbaeder.de

You'll be hard pushed to find a pool steeped in as much history as this one. Built in time for the 1936 Olympics, it's also where underwater cameras were first used to capture the divers in Leni Riefenstahl's controversial *Olympia*. Today, serious swimmers come to work out in the shadows of its massive limestone grandstands – and to say they've swum where Olympians have, of course.

BADESCHIFF

Map 2; Eichenstrasse 4, Kreuzberg; ///cheaply.staging.admit; www.arena.berlin

Though the Spree is a glorious sight, marine traffic and pollution make it a less-than-desirable swimming spot. Fortunately, the Badeschiff floating pool offers the sensation of bathing in it without going near its grotty waters, jutting out into the river at the end of a wooden pontoon. You don't come here to do lengths (it's too crowded to, anyway); rather, poolside posers laze about with cocktails, topping up tans and updating their socials. At the weekend, occasional parties pop off, with DJs soundtracking sunset and beyond.

GROSSER MÜGGELSEE

Map 6; Fürstenwalder Damm 838, Köpenick; ///views.skews.tumble

East Berlin's answer to Wannsee, the Grosser Müggelsee is the kind of lake you have no choice but to spend all day at. There's three official beach areas, so if those teens are getting too loud or you

Shh!

It's a trek to get to Kleiner Müggelsee, on the east side of its Grosser neighbour, but this keeps it firmly in the grasp of the few willing to make the effort. Once you emerge from the woods, a sloped sandy beach leads down to the lake. Bronzed couples and families come to this hidden spot for some quiet time, cooling off in the little lake's calm waters.

don't fancy sunbathing in the nude, you've got options. You've also got pedalo and boat rentals, a huge surrounding forest to hike or bike around and clear, refreshing water to dip into. Lush.

» Don't leave without climbing the Müggelturm, a GDR tower offering beautiful panoramic views over the lake.

PLÖTZENSEE

Map 6; Nordufer 26, Wedding; ///dish.dean.tens

It's early afternoon when the texts start bouncing round the group chat, weighing up a post-work trip to Plötzensee. No one ever resists. Not only is the central bathing beach on the western shore easy to reach by bike, it's a laidback spot to cool off and engage in some uninhibited sunbathing, thanks to a friendly FKK section. The carefree vibes ramp up a notch at the weekend, when DJs provide a soundtrack of summery tunes for volleyball matches on the sand.

STRANDBAD WANNSEE

Map 6; Wannseebadweg 25, Wannsee; ///dime.travels.jolly

Opened in 1907, Strandbad Wannsee was built as a summer retreat for boiling Berliners to flee city heat. A century on and it still seems like the whole of Berlin packs their swimmers and flocks to this lakeshore when the sun's out. Kids dart between giant sandcastles and friends sinking pints on covered beach chairs, occasionally tumbling over an inflatable dinghy fresh out of the water. Despite the frenzy, everyone's deeply chilled by the lazy holiday vibes, only heading back home once the sun has fully disappeared.

Alfresco Activities

*It might appear chill and sedate, but Berlin is a city
that's constantly on the move – much like its locals.
Countless waterways, forest-like parks and sporty
venues turn the city into an adventure playground.*

ERIKA HESS EISSTADION

Map 5; Müllerstrasse 185, Wedding;
///select.tenders.glorious; (030) 4690 7955

Unless an arctic snap freezes the city's lakes, this outdoor rink is
one of the few places locals will consider for a winter ice skating
session. It's a simple set-up, where lively tunes play over the PA
system, the soundtrack to friends falling about while the occasional
pro pirouettes past gracefully. When you need a break, warm up
with the dads by the snack stand and watch it all play out.

BERLINER MAUERWEG

Map 6; start at Pier Wannsee; ///battling.savers.canine;
www.berlin.de/mauer/en/wall-trail

Every Saturday, keen cyclists don their helmets and embark on their
next leg of the Berlin Wall Trail, tracing the old border between East
and West. Unless you've got thighs like Chris Hoy, it's too ambitious

to tackle the 160-km loop in one go, so most people bike it in stages. Our advice? Take the S-Bahn to Wannsee, cross the lake by ferry to Kladow, then ride the trail to Staaken. Since the route is signposted, all you need to focus on is admiring the enchanted forest and looking out for the odd frontier relics and memorials along the way.

>> Don't leave without stopping when you reach Gross Glienicke to cool off with an ice cream from Seeperle and a dip in the lake.

NATUR-PARK SCHÖNEBERGER SÜDGELÄNDE

Map 6; Prellerweg 47–9, Schöneberg; ///grants.wonderfully.impulse; (030) 700 906 710

Tucked away in Schöneberg lies this gem: disused railway land turned jungle-like nature reserve, overrun with industrial ruins, modern art and lush greenery. Power walkers and Sunday strollers meander the raised metal pathways, weaving through a tangle of trees and bushes, accompanied by singing birds and buzzing bees.

Yoga is big business in Berlin, but it's not all studio sessions. For those in the know, the outdoor pool Badeschiff *(p178)* is the best place to find Zen on summer mornings. Nothing beats the sound of water lapping at your feet as you do sun salutations balanced on a paddle board (yep, it's the ultimate workout). Check the website for times.

Solo, Pair, Crowd

After a lone urban adventure? Or want to let loose in natural surrounds? There's plenty to keep you occupied.

FLYING SOLO
Take off

Get yourself up to Tempelhof's *(p169)* former airfield at dawn and you'll have the place to yourself. Running by the enormous terminal building is an invigorating start to any day.

IN A PAIR
Pedal the prom

Grab your bikes and set off for a Spree-side cycle along Rummelsburg's Zillepromenade. Head towards Rummelsburger Ufer for sweeping views over the river and watch the sunset with your beau. Romantic, right?

FOR A CROWD
Flotilla fun

Rent a motorized float, aka *Flotte*, and head out with the gang on the River Havel at Spandau. Get your DJ mate to bring their decks and enjoy a boogie with a BBQ on the water – a Berlin summer pastime.

BEACH VOLLEYBALL AT BEACH61

Map 4; Park am Gleisdreieck, Kreuzberg; ///entry.doped.assemble;
www.beach61.de

This sandy arena is a weeknight favourite for competitive colleagues
come summer. Courts get booked up fast – especially around dusk,
when the sight of the sun setting over Potsdamer Platz in the distance
is enough to distract you from that serve. When you're all volleyed out,
it's straight to the beach bar for some post-match banter.

STAND-UP PADDLEBOARDING ON THE SPREE RIVER

Map 2; Eichenstrasse 4, Kreuzberg; ///family.voice.escapes;
www.standupclub.de

Judging by the number of boarders on the Spree in the summer, Berlin
is all for the SUPing craze. Friends work their core while seeing their
beloved city from a new perspective – nothing beats floating right
up to Jonathan Borofsky's giant *Molecule Man* standing in the river.

NEU-VENEDIG

Map 6; Rialtoring, Köpenick; ///doped.police.watches

New Venice might be smaller than its Adriatic namesake, but it's
equally as enchanting. Renting a kayak and exploring this little idyll
is pure bliss, its lily-lined waterways and romantic bridges a world
away from the tourist barges steaming the nearby Müggelspree.
» Don't leave without paddling up the river to the Müggelseefischerei
for a smoked fish sandwich and a shandy by the water.

Nearby Getaways

*Berliners couldn't be more proud of their
hometown, but with historic towns and miles of
countryside to explore on their doorstep, indulging
in a weekend getaway or two is only right.*

SPREEWALD

1-hour train from Berlin-Ostbahnhof; www.spreewald.de

Picture this: streets peppered with rustic farmhouses, tree-lined
canals dotted with rowing boats, Renaissance castles harking back
to simpler times. Welcome to Spreewald, the day trip Berliners roll
out when they're needing a good gulp of fresh air and traditional

charm. That's exactly what's to be found in this UNESCO-listed region, one of 15 biosphere reserves in Germany where unique plants and wildlife thrive. A word on the latter: pack insect repellent so you won't be swatting mosquitoes as you row down the water.

>> **Don't leave without** crunching into a tangy *Spreewaldgurke*. Locals proudly sell these beloved EU-protected gherkins from enormous wooden barrels called *Gurkenfässer*.

JÜTERBOG

1-hour train from Berlin Hauptbahnhof; www.jueterbog.eu

Jüterbog clearly didn't get the memo about turning its abandoned buildings into cool galleries, but that's exactly why intrepid explorers can't get enough of this small town. It used to act as one of the Red Army's biggest East German military installations, and its deserted buildings are a goldmine for photographers, who come to snap the eerie Soviet murals still intact. Be vigilant: decaying remains and holes in the ground abound.

LIEPNITZSEE

1-hour train and bus from Berlin-Gesundbrunnen

Berlin has tons of lakes, but if you want a proper wild swimming experience (without the crowds), you need to head further afield. Hidden away in the forest by Wandlitz, Liepnitzsee's glassy waters are a refreshing sight after a short hike through the beeches. An inviting islet in the middle of the lake attracts campers and swimmers looking to cool off with a pint in the sun-dappled beer garden.

NEURUPPIN

1.5-hour train from Berlin Hauptbahnhof

It doesn't get more quaint than this. Known colloquially as "the most Prussian of all Prussian towns", Neuruppin is pure charm, with cobbled streets, pretty gardens and traditional market squares. Better still, the thermal baths at Fontane Therme are perfect for resting tired feet after a scenic stroll through the nearby centre.

POTSDAM

40-minute train from Berlin Hauptbahnhof; www.en.potsdam.de

Despite what they say about Neuruppin, Potsdam is really the quintessential Prussian postcard. Grand palaces, tree-lined promenades and market squares make this town a classic day out when Berliners need to entertain history-loving parents. The place they always head to first? Frederick the Great's summer residence, Sanssouci, its regal Rococo architecture, extravagant follies and manicured gardens giving Versailles a run for its money.

» Don't leave without visiting Filmpark Babelsberg, the world's oldest film studio, to learn about Germany's golden age of film.

BAD SAAROW

1.5-hour train from Berlin Hauptbahnhof; www.therme.bad-saarow.de

Come winter, there's nothing a Berliner loves more than a spa day. And some serious pampering goes down at SaarowTherme, a large resort plonked atop the mineral-rich thermal springs that make the town of Bad Saarow famous. After hitting the main indoor-outdoor

Visit the Brotback Sauna at Saarow-Therme, where bread is baked at various time during the day. | pool, blissed-out visitors in bathrobes float between multiple saunas and treatment rooms, pausing for cocktails on the roof terrace.

PFAUENINSEL

1.5-hour train and tram from Hauptbahnhof; www.museumspark.de

Yes, it's within city limits, but Pfaueninsel (aka Peacock Island) is the definitive escape for romantics. No shock: the island gets its name from the resident peacocks parading their plumage around this little paradise. Beyond the birds, everything's delightfully dreamy. The main landmark, a white castle made of wood, was built by pleasure-loving Fredrich Wilhelm II for amorous encounters with his mistress; in the landscaped gardens, floral notes and love fill the air.

LEIPZIG

1.5-hour train from Berlin Hauptbahnhof; www.leipzig.travel

If Berliners could live in another German city, they'd choose Leipzig – better known as "Hypezig", given the hype that it's been afforded by the media over the last decade. And this small city certainly lives up to its stellar rep as a hotbed for creativity, an epicentre for cool start-ups and an affordable place to put down roots. And just think, if you did move, you'd have all this: contemporary galleries housed in former industrial spaces, the most vegan-friendly spots you'll find in Germany, and a pulsing techno scene thanks to fresh clubs like Institut für Zukunft. No wonder it's also called "the better Berlin".

A day exploring
idyllic Grunewald

You might not expect to find a sprawling forest in cosmopolitan Berlin, but just a short journey southwest of the centre lie the dense woodlands of Grunewald. Once a retreat for the rich, Grunewald is the domain of all manner of city slickers nowadays. Come the weekend, locals head here to zone out, crisscrossing the woodland on labyrinthine paths and absorbing the tranquil rustle of leaves and birdsong. Bring a packed lunch to keep you going and prepare to get lost in this magical, leafy wonderland.

B5

Slav prince Jaczo is said to have hung his shield here after converting to Christianity; the **Schildhorn-Denkmal** *is a monument to him.*

Havel

1. Berlin-Grunewald
Am Bahnhof
Grunewald, Grunewald
///carrots.december.paper

2. Teufelsberg
Teufelsseechaussee 10,
Grunewald; www.
teufelsberg-berlin.de
///roofs.flaked.exists

3. Teufelssee
Grunewald
///torn.restless.kinds

4. Biergarten am Grunewaldturm
Havelchaussee 61,
Grunewald; www.kaiser
garten-grunewald.de
///deaf.shaver.watched

Jagdschloss Grunewald
///miracle.lodge.clutter

Drachensberg
///slap.monopoly.chase

Schildhorn-Denkmal
///gain.tenders.projects

Rest your feet at BIERGARTEN AM GRUNEWALDTURM
Unwind with a drink at this chilled beer garden, nestled beside the Grunewald Tower, before getting a bus home.

HAVELCHAUSSEE

Havel

0 kilometres   1

0 miles   1

HEERSTRASSE

Walk up
TEUFELSBERG
Scale this artificial
mountain and you'll find a
run-down, graffitied NSA
listening station. Here,
sweeping vistas await.

When it snows,
Drachensberg – *a heap
of wartime rubble to
rival Teufelsberg – teems
with locals sledding
down its slopes.*

2

GRUNEWALD

3

Cool off at
TEUFELSSEE
Throw down a rug beside
this shady lake and enjoy
your picnic before taking a
dip (bathing suits optional).

1

Arrive at
BERLIN-
GRUNEWALD
Once off the S-Bahn,
pause for thought
at the Mahnmal
Gleis 17 memorial, a
platform from where
over 50,000 Jews
were deported.

A115

Grunewald

Grunewald-
see

Built in 1543,
Jagdschloss Grunewald
*is the oldest preserved
castle in Berlin, and
gave the surrounding
forest its name.*

A115

DAHLEM

With a little research and preparation, this city will feel like a home away from home. Check out these websites to ensure a healthy, safe stay in Berlin.

Berlin
DIRECTORY

SAFE SPACES

Berlin is a welcoming and inclusive city, but should you feel uneasy or want to find your community, there are a host of spaces catering to different genders, sexualities, demographics and religions.

www.berlin-aidshilfe.de
Contact point and counselling service for HIV-positive people.

www.berlin-judentum.de
An all-encompassing community centre for Berlin's Jewish communities.

www.blackbrownberlin.com
A curated online platform with a guide to Berlin's Black- and Brown-owned businesses and events listings.

www.lesbenberatung-berlin.de
Counselling centre for lesbian women.

www.village.berlin/vision
Modern community centre for gay, bisexual, trans and queer men to connect.

HEALTH

Healthcare in Germany isn't free to all so make sure you have comprehensive health insurance; emergency healthcare is covered by the European Health Insurance Card (EHIC) for EU residents and the UK Global Health Insurance Card (GHIC) for those from the UK. If you do need medical assistance, there are many pharmacies and hospitals.

www.akberlin.de
A list of pharmacies grouped by district and open outside of usual hours.

www.berlin-health-excellence.com
Information on local services and hospitals around Berlin.

www.charite.de
Berlin's main central hospital with a 24-hour emergency room.

www.en.berliner-krankenhaus verzeichnis.de
A directory of hospitals that provide treatments for particular ailments (note that a doctor's referral will be needed).

www.kvberlin.de
General advice on the health system with emergency numbers and a search engine to find English-speaking doctors.

TRAVEL SAFETY ADVICE

Berlin is generally a very safe city. Before you travel – and while you're here – always keep tabs on the latest regulations in Germany.

www.auswaertiges-amt.de
Most recent updates on entry and residency from the foreign office.

www.berlin.de
Latest news from Berlin and a list of emergency service numbers.

www.bundesregierung.de
The German Federal Government website, the first port of call for COVID-19 regulations and current issues.

www.internetwache-polizei-berlin.de
Official police website for reporting crimes.

ACCESSIBILITY

Berlin is a highly accessible city, and laws and regulations are constantly pushing for improvements. These resources will help make your journeys go smoothly.

www.absv.org
Charitable association offering practical advice for the blind and sight-impaired.

www.bvg.de
Official transport website with an accessible journey planner and information on broken lifts.

www.vbb.de
Free bus and train escort services can be booked with the Berlin and Brandenburg transport agency.

www.visitberlin.de
Official resource for visiting Berlin, with lists of accessible venues, restaurants and attractions as well as tips.

www.wheelmap.org
Find wheelchair accessible places in the city on a map.

ABOUT THE ILLUSTRATOR

Mantas Tumosa

Creative designer and illustrator Mantas moved from his home country of Lithuania to London back in 2011. By day, he's busy creating bold, minimalistic illustrations that tell a story – such as the gorgeous cover of this book. By night, he's dreaming of adventures away, catching up on the basketball and cooking Italian food (which he can't get enough of).

Main Contributors Marlen Jacobshagen, Alexander Rennie, Barbara Woolsey

Senior Editor Lucy Richards

Senior Designer Tania Gomes

Project Editor Zoë Rutland

Project Art Editor Ankita Sharma

Proofreader Stephanie Smith

Senior Cartographic Editor Casper Morris

Cartography Manager Suresh Kumar

Cartographer Ashif

Jacket Designer Tania Gomes

Jacket Illustrator Mantas Tumosa

Senior Production Editor Jason Little

Senior Production Controller Stephanie McConnell

Managing Editor Hollie Teague

Managing Art Editor Bess Daly

Art Director Maxine Pedliham

Publishing Director Georgina Dee

First edition 2022

Published in Great Britain by Dorling Kindersley Limited,
DK, One Embassy Gardens, 8 Viaduct Gardens,
London SW11 7BW.

The authorised representative in the EEA is
Dorling Kindersley Verlag GmbH. Arnulfstr. 124,
80636 Munich, Germany.

Published in the United States by DK Publishing,
1450 Broadway, Suite 801, New York, NY 10018.

Copyright © 2022 Dorling Kindersley Limited
A Penguin Random House Company
22 23 24 25 10 9 8 7 6 5 4 3 2 1

A CIP catalog record for this book is available from the British Library.

A catalog record for this book is available from the Library of Congress.

ISSN: 1542 1554
ISBN: 978 0 2415 2386 5

Printed and bound in Latvia.

www.dk.com

A NOTE FROM DK EYEWITNESS

The world is fast-changing and it's keeping us folk at DK Eyewitness on our toes. We've worked hard to ensure that this edition of Berlin Like a Local is up-to-date and reflects today's favourite places but we know that standards shift, venues close and new ones pop up in their place. So, if you notice something has closed, we've got something wrong or left something out, we want to hear about it. Please drop us a line at travelguides@dk.com